MEXICO THROUGH
MY KITCHEN WINDOW

BY **MARIA A. DE CARBIA**
EDITED AND TESTED BY HELEN CORBITT

Mexico Th

My Kitchen

...rugh Window

WITH A COLLECTION OF TYPICALLY TEXAN
MEXICAN RECIPES PREPARED ESPECIALLY
FOR THIS BOOK BY HELEN CORBITT

Illustrated by Luis Betanzos

HOUGHTON MIFFLIN COMPANY BOSTON
THE RIVERSIDE PRESS CAMBRIDGE

Third Printing   W

The Riverside Press
CAMBRIDGE · MASSACHUSETTS
PRINTED IN THE U.S.A.

The Author

Mrs. Maria A. de Carbia was born in Mexico City of Spanish and French grandparents. She was educated in a French convent and later studied home economics and cooking both in the United States and in Mexico.

She published her first cookbook in 1936 under the *nom de plume* of Marichu, which means Little Mary, the name that her Basque grandmother used to call her. The title of her first book was *Marichu Va a la Cocina* (Little Mary Goes to the Kitchen) and subsequently she has published several more, one with her impressions of different countries of Europe, the Near East and Egypt.

Besides her interest in cooking she has devoted herself to flower arranging and gardening and has given lectures in her country on these subjects and also on herbs and spices, on which she also has published a book. She is Home Economics Consultant for Walter Thompson, S.A., of Mexico.

This is Maria Carbia's book. It expresses her charm and the intangible something that makes this book worth your consideration. At first I was not sure her combination of ingredients would be acceptable to my palate, but while many of the flavors were new to me, I found myself going back for a second taste. Best of all, these recipes are economical, with an interesting quality to them and not just the same old way of extending a pound of meat to feed the multitude. For this alone it should be in your collection of usable cookbooks.

In extending the scope of this Mexican food story I am including some favorite North of the Border foods that Texans and others have found to their taste, which in their "breezy Texas" way they call "Mexican Food."

I have edited this book with a hands-off approach. Maria's charm cannot be edited. Do, however, be sensible and use an electric blender or food chopper in place of a mortar and pestle or a metate. No one — today — is physically up to such an exercise.

HELEN CORBITT

Contents

Some Facts About Food in Mexico

THERE IS in foreign countries the erroneous thought that Mexican people in general eat everything with tortillas and chile. In Mexico City and the main cities in the country at good restaurants and in the homes of well-to-do people, the food is more or less international.

People enjoy once or twice a week an *antojo*, as we call the tacos, enchiladas, mole, or other typical food, but only as one of the dishes in the menu, and very seldom do we serve what is known as a Mexican Dinner, which includes several of these dishes. It may be done in a ranch country home or for the benefit of foreign visitors.

I remember once in California I was visiting a friend who had been to Mexico several times and had enjoyed typical Mexican food very much, and she told me: "You know, Mrs. Carbia, when

I invite friends whom I really want to please, I serve them Mexican rice, pork in adobo sauce, enchiladas, mole, tacos and refried beans, in the same meal."

"Heavens!" I said, "you must give them bicarbonate of soda for dessert."

Middle-class people eat almost every day a soup or rice accompanied by a sauce made of chopped tomatoes, onion, chile, and sometimes avocado, a dish of meat with potatoes which is sometimes cooked in chile sauce, and beans.

Unfortunately the Indians in the country, and the poor people in the cities, eat very little meat and eggs. Their meal consists of beans, chile sauce, and tortillas.

Chile contains vitamins. The corn with which the tortillas are made is boiled with lime, and the beans contain iron and proteins. Maybe that accounts for the good teeth the Indians have, their abundant hair, and their fortitude that is in no relation with the little food they eat.

There are hundreds of varieties of "chiles" in Mexico, from the tiniest and very hot ones like the "Piquin" (the size of a small pea) to the biggest sweet red or green pimentos.

Chiles are very decorative. I have a plant in my home in Cuernavaca that bears small chiles of different color in the same branch. They are the size of an olive and quite round, so the bush when full of chiles resembles a Christmas tree with its colored balls.

There is another variety that is orange and round, the size of a crab apple, and it grows like a vine. When planted near a plumbago vine with its light blue flowers, the combination is striking. Perfect complementary colors!

I am here describing the most popular of fresh, dried, and canned varieties.

Chile Serrano (Green pepper from the Sierra)
Small elongated green chile. One of the most popular in Mexico. In the homes of the poor, in

many middle-class homes, and at the servants' tables, it is served at mealtime in a small dish. Each person takes them, to chop in his soup, rice, or meat. It is also chopped raw in the guacamole and tacos. If boiled in the rice or other dish, it gives a very tasty flavor. Care should be taken not to let it break, as then it makes food very hot.

It is sold in the markets in colorful heaps, as it is sometimes red and also yellow.

Chile Cuaresmeno (Chile for Lent)

Larger than the Serrano, it is also very hot. It is very popular in cans, called also Jalapeño. It comes whole or in strips marinated in oil and vinegar.

Chile Poblano (Chile from Puebla)

It resembles the green pepper but it is hot, although if well prepared it is soft and palatable. This is the way to prepare it.

1. Toast well the chile over a slow flame, until black spots appear over the whole surface. Soak immediately in cold water and peel off the skin.

2. Open on one side and remove seeds and strings attached to the sides of the chile, called veins in Mexico.

3. Soak in water with salt and vinegar, if possible overnight.

It is now ready to use in Chiles Rellenos (Stuffed Peppers) or to cut in strips called *rajas* or to chop for different dishes.

This is the chile I have substituted in the recipes with green pepper.

Now it is being sold in cans very well prepared and ready to use. Eventually it will be sold in the U.S.A. for the people who like a little hot flavor.

DRIED CHILES

Pasilla Chile (Raisin chile)
Green when fresh, it is generally used dried and then it is wrinkled and a dark-red color. It is used soaked and ground, and used in combination with other dried chiles, for various *moles* or sauces.

Chile Ancho (Large or broad chile)
This is the Poblano when dry. It has become wrinkled and red. It is used soaked and ground for several moles and sauces.

Chile Mulato (Mulatto pepper)
It is the darker of the red dry chiles and it is used as in the two previous ones.

Chipotle Smaller than the other dry chiles, it is also red and used most of the time prepared in vinegar. It is very tasty. One piece is generally put in the tortas, the pambacitos, and the tostadas.

CANNED CHILES

The most popular chiles sold in cans are:

Serranos en escabeche
Small green peppers, already described. In cans they are pickled or marinated.

Chiles largos en escabeche
Long chiles, light green in color. They are also

pickled or marinated. Used to garnish dishes like the Pescado a la Veracruzana (Fish Veracruz Style), Bacalao a la Vizcaina (Dry Cod Viscay), or Flambre (Cold Meat Platter).

Chipotles en vinagre
Already described with the dry chiles.

Poblanos (Puebla peppers)
New in the market. Well prepared without oil or vinegar but ready to stuff. They come also in strips to use in various dishes or to grind for sauces.

Mole It comes in powder to be fried or diluted for sauce. Other are used in paste form.

They all come with instructions on how to use.

BEANS

We have also a great variety of beans: Black tiny ones, light yellow ones — Canario (Canary bird); brown ones called *Bayos* (palomino color); big brown ones called Bayo Gordo (Fat Palomino); red, purple, and of course the white, resembling the navy bean. There is one enormous variety called Ayocote that is always cooked in mole sauce.

CORN

There is also a great variety of corn, as in the U.S.A. We eat it fresh on the cob, ground in many dishes, and fresh-cut from the cob. When dry it is ground and made into a meal and used for atole (beverage), tamales, and of course tortillas.

MEXICO THROUGH
MY KITCHEN WINDOW

Tortillas

THE WONDERFUL ART OF MAKING TORTILLAS

Just as in Africa the tom-tom greets the ear of the wandering stranger, in Mexico the sound of the clapping hands of the Indian woman greets the ear of the wandering tourist, especially through the country roads and small villages.

This is the sight we see:

A small adobe hut. Several children running about, one of them sleeping in a wooden box, a few chickens (or maybe pigs) keeping company. An Indian woman bent over the *metate*. This is a small, low, inclined table made of porous stone. It has a handle or, rather, a rolling pin, made of the same stone with which she grinds the corn, previously soaked for several hours in hot limewater. The result is a meal fine and smooth in texture. The woman takes a nut-size ball, flattens it and claps it between her hands, producing the most wonderfully even pancakes in size and shape. Dozens of them, all alike as two drops of water.

She bakes these pancakes on a round tin sheet over a wood fire. When they are golden brown on both sides but still soft, she places them in a square reed basket lined with a clean embroidered doily.

Tortillas have been the Indian bread for hundreds of years, and the rest of the meal most of the time is beans with chile. The drink is *pulque,* the liquor extracted from the agave plant. The legend about the origin of this drink is poetical, and the drink itself would not be so bad if it were kept clean and taken without abuse. Unfortunately both conditions are lacking among the lower class of people.

The middle- and high-class people eat tortillas instead of bread once in a while, "for a change," especially accompanying some chile dishes, but they use them mainly for the confection of some fancy dishes as enchiladas.

By the way, if it is true that the metates are used less and less by younger generations, especially in the big cities where liquidizers and blenders are taking their place, such interesting gadgets are being used by some young sophisticates, especially in the houses of very modern Mexican architecture, for other uses that are a far cry from what they were intended for — such as seats in front of the television, or around a low table. Sometimes they are provided with velvet cushions and even with silk tassels.

TORTILLAS — BASIC RECIPE

White cornmeal	½ cup
Salt	½ teaspoon
Milk	½ cup
Cooking oil	2 tablespoons
Eggs	3

Mix all the ingredients.

Grease and heat small frying pan and place in it one tablespoon of the mixture, running it well so as to form a round pancake. When done on one side, turn. Keep hot and soft on platter over hot water. They can be eaten as tortillas **or** used in tacos, enchiladas, etc. For 16 tortillas.

TOMATO AND CHICKEN ENCHILADAS
(*Enchiladas de Tomate Rojo*)

Tortillas	Basic recipe
Processed cheese	1 package
Avocado	1
Onion	1
Shredded chicken (cooked)	1 cup

SAUCE

Cooking fat	
Minced onion	2 tablespoons
Minced garlic	1 clove (optional)
Tomato sauce	2½ cups
Chili sauce or powder	1 tablespoon
Minced parsley	1 tablespoon
Salt	To taste

Melt fat, fry onion and garlic; when soft add tomato sauce,

chili, and parsley. Season well with salt and cook gently until thick.

Have a hot platter ready. Take each pancake and dip it in sauce, fill with some shredded chicken, and roll. Place on platter. After all rolls are on platter pour the rest of the sauce over them. Keep warm in the oven until ready to serve (although it is advisable to make them as close to serving time as possible). Garnish with crumbled processed cheese, avocado slices and onion rings. Instead of the chicken, any leftover meat may be used. Provolone cheese can be used instead of the processed cheese. For 8, allowing 2 tortillas per person.

MOLE ENCHILADAS

Tortillas	Basic recipe
Mole sauce	1 cup
Chicken meat	1 cup
Sliced onion	1
Toasted sesame seeds	3 tablespoons
Radish roses	8

Make mole sauce according to recipe given in POULTRY section of this book or use canned mole sauce. Follow directions for making Tomato Enchiladas and garnish the plate with onion rings, toasted sesame seeds and radish roses. For 8.

SANTA CLARA ENCHILADAS

Tortillas	Basic recipe
Sauce	As for Mole Enchiladas
Eggs	2
Fat	2 tablespoons
Ground pork	½ pound
Ground veal	½ pound
Chopped tomatoes	½ cup
Almonds	18
Raisins	20
Salt	To taste

Make sauce as for Mole Enchiladas. Beat egg whites until stiff. Add yolks one by one, beating after each addition.

Melt fat, add meat, and when brown, add chopped tomatoes, chopped blanched almonds and raisins. Cook until very thick.

Dip tortillas in sauce, fill with meat, and roll. Place layer of rolls in buttered baking dish, cover with a little of the sauce and some beaten egg. Repeat layers, finishing with a layer of egg. Bake in oven until brown. For 8.

BANANA ENCHILADAS (*Enchiladas de Plátano*)

Tortillas	Basic recipe
Bananas	4
Butter	3 tablespoons
Sauce	As for Mole Enchiladas

Cut bananas in thick slices and then in two crosswise. Fry in butter. Dip each tortilla in sauce. Roll a piece of fried banana in each, place on hot platter, and cover with the rest of the sauce. Keep warm until ready to serve. For 8.

MILK AND EGG ENCHILADAS
(*Enchiladas con Huevo y Leche*)

Tortillas	Basic recipe
Tomato sauce	2½ cups
Butter	¼ cup
Soda	1 pinch
Milk	1 cup
Chili powder	1 teaspoon (optional)
Egg	1
Swiss cheese, grated	½ cup

Fry tomato sauce in butter, add soda, when thick add hot milk and chili powder. Remove from fire and add beaten egg.

Dip each tortilla in the sauce, fold, and place on hot platter. Sprinkle cheese on top. For 8.

ENCHILADAS WITH GREEN PEPPER SAUCE
(*Enchiladas en Salsa de Chile Poblano*)

Tortillas	Basic recipe
Processed cheese	1 package

SAUCE

Green peppers or canned Poblano peppers	3
Butter	¼ cup
Soda	1 pinch
Milk	2 cups
Salt	To taste

After tortillas are ready, put a slice of cheese in each, fold, and secure with a toothpick. Fry in hot fat and drain well. Then cook two or three minutes in the sauce and serve very hot.

To make the sauce, clean the peppers and boil until very soft. Grind well until reduced to a paste. Fry in the butter and add soda, then hot milk. Cook until thick. Season well. For 8.

ENCHILADAS WITH BEAN SAUCE (*Enfrijoladas*)

Tortillas	Basic recipe
Red kidney beans	1 can
Butter	2 tablespoons
Minced onion	2 tablespoons
Chili sauce	To taste
Salt	To taste
Chicken or sausage meat	1 cup
Grated cheese	1 cup

Mash beans and strain with some water or stock. Melt butter, add onion, and when soft add bean sauce and chili. Season well with salt and cook until creamy.

Butter a baking dish and place a layer of tortillas folded and filled with the meat, a layer of bean sauce and grated cheese. Repeat layers, placing cheese on top. Bake in the oven 10 to 15 minutes. For 8.

SAN LUIS ENCHILADAS (*Enchiladas de San Luis*)

Tortillas	Basic recipe
Red chili powder	1 tablespoon
Grated American cheese	3 tablespoons

FILLING

Fat	2 tablespoons
Minced onion	1 tablespoon
Chopped tomatoes	3
Green peppers or Poblano peppers	2
Processed cheese	1 3-ounce package
Salt	To taste
Melted butter	¾ cup

When batter for tortillas is ready, add chili powder and grated cheese. Make pancakes as in basic recipe.

Melt fat and add onion; when soft, add chopped tomatoes and chopped green peppers (previously cleaned and boiled). Cook until thick and add crumbled cream cheese. Remove from fire. Put a little of the filling in each pancake and fold. Butter baking dish and place enchiladas in layers, pouring some melted butter over each layer. Bake in hot oven 15 to 20 minutes. For 8.

"Mimsa" is the commercial tortilla meal available for the housewife in Mexican grocery stores.

24 TORTILLAS MADE WITH MIMSA (Tortilla Meal)

Mimsa meal	1 cup
Water	¾ to 1 cup

Mix well. Let stand at least one hour, the longer the better. Cook as in basic recipe, page 3.

TURNOVERS MADE WITH MIMSA

Mimsa meal	1 cup
Water	¾ cup
Flour	¼ cup
Salt	½ teaspoon
Melted lard or butter	1 tablespoon
Thick or sour cream	1 tablespoon
Baking powder	1 teaspoon

Mix Mimsa with water and let stand for at least an hour. Mix with the other ingredients and let stand another hour or more.

Make balls and press flat (little tortilla machines are available). Fill, and fry in hot oil. Serve hot. For 8.

CREPES (to be used as tortillas instead of bread or for making enchiladas)

Cornmeal	½ cup
Milk	½ cup
Eggs	3
Salt	½ teaspoon
Cooking oil	2 tablespoons

Combine all ingredients. Grease the frying pan for the first crepe. Pour a small amount of batter into hot frying pan — the crepes should be very thin — and cook until done, turning when brown on the first side. For 8 or 12.

SERAPE CANAPE (*Blanket*)

Cut bread slices in three and toast. Mash cream cheese and
add a little cream or milk to make a soft paste well seasoned
with salt and pepper. Spread on toast, making some lines
or depressions to imitate the serape fringe. Then start with
the color lines, forming them with very thin strips of pimento, green pepper, red or black caviar, liver paste,
smoked salmon, hard-boiled egg yolk or any other food that
can give color and taste to the canapé.

SOMBRERO CANAPE (*Mexican Hat*)

Slice bread, cut in circles, toast and spread with cream
cheese paste. With the same paste form small cones to

imitate the sombrero's top. Place thin strips of red pimento around the tops, forming the hat's band. Sprinkle a little paprika over it.

NOPAL CANAPE (*Prickly Pears*)

Cut bread slices in circles or squares. Toast and spread with liverwurst or sardine paste softened with a little cream.

Boil two green peppers for ten minutes and peel. With tiny oval cutters make ovals of different sizes (the largest being about the size of a dime). Form the cactus plant on the canapé and simulate the *tunas* (fruits) with red caviar eggs.

ORGANO CANAPE (*Candle Cactus*)

Cut bread slices in circles or squares. Spread with liverwurst.

Boil two green peppers for ten minutes and peel. Cut in long strips differing in size and rounded on the top to resemble the candle cactus. Imitate the clusters of spines with tiny black caviar eggs.

JICARA CANAPE (*Uruapan Gourd Bowl*)

Prepare small round rolls or biscuits. When done, cut in half, take out the soft part, leaving only the crusts to imitate a bowl, fry them in butter and drain on paper towel. Cover the inside, as though it were painted with black caviar. Garnish with flowers or just tiny pieces of red pimento, parsley or hard-boiled egg. You could use the prepared biscuits.

GUAJE CANAPE   (*Gourd*)

Slice brown or white bread and cut as gourds (the shape of a long pear). You can shape a round tin cutter with your fingers. Spread with pimento cheese or deviled ham. Decorate with tiny pieces of red pimento, green pepper and hard-boiled egg.

MEXICAN PIG CANAPE   (*Canapé "El Cochinito"*)

With a pig-shaped cutter (they are sold for making ginger cookies) cut bread slices, toast, and spread with pimento cheese or deviled ham. Make the eye with a tiny black pepper and the twisted tail with a thin pimento strip. You can leave the body plain or decorate it in as fancy a way as you desire, with tiny flowers or other figures made of pimento, parsley or hard-boiled egg.

AVOCADO CANAPE WITH ANCHOVY FILLETS
(*Canapé de Aguacate*)

Cut circles or squares of bread, remove crust and toast. Spread with well-seasoned avocado paste made by mashing avocado meat and adding salt, pepper, and a little olive oil. Garnish each canapé with an anchovy fillet and a strip of red pimento.

TOTOPOS   (*Tortilla Fritters*)

Totopos are squares or triangles made with tortilla, fried and used to decorate different dishes instead of the bread triangle.

On the eve of making these appetizers make the tortillas as in the basic recipe. Just after making the pancakes, cut each one in four triangles and let dry. Next day fry them in hot fat until crispy and drain on paper towel. Spread with mashed and fried red kidney beans, mixed with a little chili sauce or powder. Sprinkle with grated cheese.

TORTITAS COMPUESTAS (*Garnished Small Rolls*)

Slit tiny rolls and spread the bottom half with mashed, well-fried bean paste, then put a layer of shredded romaine with French dressing and some shredded chicken, salmon or sardines; then two or three bits of white cheese, a small avocado slice, and chili to taste. Cover with the top part of the roll. Serve cold with cocktails.

This is also a suitable party dish accompanied by tea or coffee.

AVOCADO COCKTAIL

For each cocktail

Catsup	2 tablespoons
Lemon juice	1 teaspoon
Worcestershire sauce	½ teaspoon
Tabasco sauce	2 drops
Italian vermouth	1 tablespoon
Salt	To taste
Avocado meat, cut in cubes	¼ cup

Mix all the ingredients and serve very cold in crystal glasses.

PAMBACITOS COMPUESTOS (*Garnished Rolls*)

When the rolls are made the regular size this dish is served as a typical party dish; but I have tried them as hors d'oeuvres accompanying the cocktail and they have been a success.

Make very tiny oval rolls or tiny biscuits. When baked, slit and take out the inside, leaving only the crusts forming tiny bread cases. Let dry a few hours. Near serving time fry them in hot fat and drain on paper towel.

Slice some lettuce very thin. Dice some boiled potatoes and dress both with French dressing. Slice some Vienna sausages and fry slightly in fat. Put in the bottom part of each biscuit or fried roll a little of the salad, two slices of the sausage (fried sausage meat of any kind will do), some chili powder or sauce, and a sprinkling of grated cheese. Cover with the fried top. Keep hot in the oven. Serve with cocktail and wait for the ahs and ohs of your guests.

GRAHAM BISCUITS

Graham flour	2 cups
Baking powder	4 teaspoons
Salt	½ teaspoon
Shortening	2 tablespoons
Milk	¾ cup

Combine graham flour with baking powder and salt. Add shortening and mix well. Add milk little by little. Do not handle much. Roll on floured board and cut with tiny biscuit cutter, or make little oval or round rolls by hand. Bake in hot oven about 20 minutes. Makes 24 to 30 small biscuits.

You can use this recipe for making Jicara Canapés.

FISH PANUCHOS VERACRUZ STYLE

Make tiny biscuits with above recipe. When out of the oven, slit, take out the inside dough, and fry the crusts. Drain on paper towel.

Melt a little shortening, add a little onion. When transparent, add chopped tomatoes and parsley. Cook ten minutes, then add flaked fish (fresh or canned) and cook until quite thick. I suggest tuna fish.

Mash some red kidney beans and fry the paste in fat.

Spread some mashed beans in the bottom part of the biscuits, then a layer of fish, and cover with the biscuit top. Keep hot in the oven and serve with cocktails. If the biscuits are made the regular size, they can be served for lunch or as a party or supper dish accompanied by tea or coffee.

Soups

As in many European countries, a good stock is prepared every day in Mexican kitchens. It is made with a good soupbone, carrots, turnips, leeks, herbs, etc. Sometimes it is made with meat and this is prepared the same day, or the day after, as the main luncheon dish (see Meats).

SPANISH GARLIC SOUP   (*Sopa de Ajo*)

Bread slices	6
Olive oil	3 tablespoons
Garlic	4 cloves
Hot stock or water	2 quarts
Salt and pepper	To taste
Eggs	6

Cut bread slices in four and toast in the oven.

Heat olive oil and fry garlic cloves until brown. Add hot stock or water, salt and pepper. Let boil five minutes and add toasted bread slices. Cook until bread is well soaked but not too soft.

Take out garlic cloves before serving. Place a poached egg in each soup plate and pour hot soup over it. For 8.

ELBOW MACARONI WITH SPINACH SOUP
(*Sopa de Codito con Espinaca*)

Fat	1 tablespoon
Minced onion	1 teaspoon
Minced garlic	1 clove (optional)
Tomato pulp	½ cup
Stock	2 quarts
Boiled elbow macaroni	2 cups
Minced boiled spinach	½ cup
Salt and pepper	To taste

Melt fat. Fry onion, garlic and tomato pulp. When well fried, add strained stock and let boil five minutes. Add the cooked elbow macaroni and the chopped spinach. Cook ten minutes.

Grated cheese should be added when serving. For 8.

MEXICAN VERMICELLI SOUP (*Sopa de Fideos*)

Stock	2 quarts
Fat	2 tablespoons
Vermicelli	½ package (8-ounce)
Minced onion	1 teaspoon
Minced garlic	1 clove (optional)
Tomato pulp or purée	½ cup
Minced parsley	1 teaspoon
Salt and pepper	To taste

Have stock ready. Melt fat and fry vermicelli until golden brown. Add onion, garlic and tomato. Cook five minutes. Add strained stock, salt, pepper and parsley. Cook until vermicelli is tender. For 8.

POTATO AND LEEK SOUP (*Sopa de Poro y Papa*)

Potatoes	1 pound
Leeks	3
Fat	2 tablespoons
Minced onion	1 teaspoon
Minced garlic	1 clove (optional)
Tomato pulp	½ cup
Stock	2 quarts
Salt and pepper	To taste

Peel and cut potatoes in narrow strips. Put in cold salted water. Slice leeks.

Melt fat and fry potatoes (wiped with clean cloth) and leeks. When potatoes are transparent, add onion, garlic and tomato. When this is well fried, add strained stock. Cook gently until potatoes are done. For 8.

GREEN PUREE OF RICE AND CHICKEN
(*Sopa de Arroz Verde con Pollo*)

Chicken breast	1
Chicken stock	1 quart
Rice	½ pound
Parsley	1 bunch
Salt and pepper	To taste

Boil chicken breast in enough water to make the stock. Boil the rice separately and when soft pass through food chopper with enough parsley to make a pale green paste. Pass through a sieve with the stock and season well with salt and pepper.

Just before serving add the diced chicken breast. Chicken livers may be used instead of the breast. For 4.

SOUP WITH CHICKEN AND POTATO DUMPLINGS
(*Sopa de Bolitas de Pollo y Papa*)

Stock	2 quarts
Chicken breast	1
Potatoes	3
Minced onion	1 teaspoon
Eggs	2
Salt and pepper	To taste
Butter	1 tablespoon
Flour	1 tablespoon

Boil the potatoes, mash, and add chicken breast, ground, minced onion, beaten eggs and salt and pepper. Make into small dumplings.

Melt butter and brown the flour. When smooth add the stock and let simmer for a few minutes. Add the dumplings and serve very hot. For 8.

CUSTARD SOUP (*Sopa de Jericalla*)

Eggs	4
Stock	2 quarts
Cornstarch	1 teaspoon
Parsley	1 tablespoon
Salt and pepper	To taste
Nutmeg	1 dash
Sugar	1 teaspoon
Sherry wine	¼ cup

Beat the four eggs for a few minutes, add gradually a cup of lukewarm stock, cornstarch, parsley, and season well with salt, pepper and nutmeg. Put in top of double boiler until custard is set. Brown the sugar in a saucepan until dark and add to the rest of the hot stock and also the sherry wine. A few minutes before serving add the custard cut in cubes. For 8.

BLACK RICE SOUP (*Sopa de Arroz Negro*)

Red kidney beans	1 large can
Shortening	1 tablespoon
Minced onion	1 tablespoon
Rice	½ cup
Tomato sauce	½ cup
Salt and pepper	To taste
Water	2 quarts

Mash beans and pass through sieve with some of the water. Melt shortening, add onion and washed rice. When it begins to get brown, add tomato sauce, salt and pepper. Cook ten minutes. Add beans and water. Cook gently until rice is done and creamy. For 8.

SPANISH CABBAGE SOUP
(*Sopa Española de Col*)

Diced bacon	¼ pound
Minced onion	1 teaspoon
Garlic	1 clove
Sliced leeks (the white part)	½ cup
Sliced white cabbage	1 cup
Sliced red cabbage	1 cup
Tomato sauce	½ cup
Stock or water	1½ quarts
Bay leaf	1
Potatoes	2
Peppercorns	2
Clove	1
Salt and pepper	To taste
Vinegar	1 teaspoon

Put bacon in pan over fire. When fat is melted, add minced onion, minced garlic and leeks. When they begin to brown, add sliced cabbage and, shortly after, tomato sauce. After five minutes add the stock and bay leaf and cook gently half an hour. Add the potatoes cut in cubes and continue cooking gently until potatoes are done. Finally add the ground peppercorns and clove, salt, pepper and vinegar. Serve very hot. For 8.

CUCUMBER SOUP   (*Sopa de Pepino*)

Cucumbers	3
Potatoes	2
Butter	3 tablespoons
Minced onion	1 tablespoon
Flour	1 tablespoon
Stock	2 quarts
Small peas	1 can
Minced parsley	1 tablespoon
Salt and pepper	To taste

Peel and cube the cucumbers and the potatoes. Melt half of the butter and fry onion until transparent. Add cucumbers and potatoes and sprinkle with the flour. When it begins to brown add two cups of the stock.

Mash half of the peas and pass through sieve with the remaining stock. Add to soup and season well. Just before serving add the peas, parsley and the rest of the butter. For 8.

GREEN SOUP   (*Sopa Verde*)

Boiled spinach	1 cup
Peas	1 large can
Butter	1 tablespoon
Minced onion	1 tablespoon
Stock	2 quarts
Salt and pepper	To taste
Ginger powder	To taste (optional)
Prunes	6
Boiled ham, chopped	¼ pound

Blend the spinach and half of the peas and pass through sieve with a little water.

Melt butter and add onion; when soft, add to the soup with the stock. Cook 10 minutes. Add spices, sliced prunes, chopped ham and whole peas. Serve hot. For 8.

LENTEN CONVENT SOUP (*Sopa del Convento*)

Spanish chick-peas	½ pound
Soda	1 pinch
Onion	1
Bay leaf	1
Parsley	1 sprig
Cloves	2
Olive oil	3 tablespoons
Hard-boiled egg yolks	3
Salt and pepper	To taste

Soak the chick-peas overnight. Next morning put in pan with 2 quarts of water, and boil for 1 hour. Add the soda, continue boiling for some time and then drain in colander. After they are skinned put back in pan with one of the onions, bay leaf, parsley and cloves. Add water to cover and continue boiling.

When the onion is soft, mince a raw onion and fry in the olive oil. Remove half of the chick-peas from the boiling water and combine with both the fried and boiled onions, the oil, and the three egg yolks. Mash well, adding a little of the water in which the other peas are boiling, and add paste to the boiling pot. Cook until peas are tender.

If not for Lent a bouillon cube or some meat extract may be added for flavor.

It can also be made with lima beans. Or with bacon fat and served with minced crisp bacon. For 8.

VALENCIAN SOUP   (*Sopa Valenciana*)

Large potatoes	2
Cabbage	½ small head
Onion	1 tablespoon
Minced parsley	1 tablespoon
Olive oil	3 tablespoons
Tomatoes	1 small can
Raw ham	¼ pound
Salt and pepper	To taste
Stock	1½ quarts
Boiled peas	1 cup
Rice	3 tablespoons

Peel and dice potatoes and slice cabbage. Put with minced onion in the hot oil. When onion is soft add tomatoes, ham, salt and pepper and water. Boil for 30 minutes, then add peas, minced parsley and rice. Cook until rice is done. For 6 or 8.

SOUP QUEEN OF MONTEVIDEO
(*Sopa Reina de Montevideo*)

Butter	¼ cup
Onion	1
Corn	1 small can
Cooked spinach	½ cup
Water	1 pint
Cornstarch	1 tablespoon
Milk	1 pint
Salt and pepper	To taste
Egg yolks	2

Melt butter, add onion. When soft, add corn and chopped

spinach, then water and boil 15 minutes. Dilute cornstarch in the milk and add to the soup and cook until it thickens a little. Season well.

Near dinnertime add the two yolks diluted in a little of the soup. Serve hot. For 4 or 6.

BLACK BEAN SOUP

Dried black beans	1½ cups
Water	3 quarts
Onion	1
Oil	2 tablespoons
Salt	To taste
Shortening	2 tablespoons
Tortillas	3
Hard summer sausage	1 3-inch piece
Tomato purée	3 tablespoons
Minced garlic	1 small clove (optional)
Minced parsley	2 tablespoons
Chili powder	To taste
Grated cheese	To taste

Pick over and wash beans. Soak overnight in water. Next morning discard the beans that float and place the rest in large kettle with water, onion, oil and salt and boil until very soft. (Pressure cooker may be used.)

Mash beans and pass through sieve, or use liquidizer.

Heat shortening (lard, vegetable shortening or oil) and fry tortillas lightly, then sausage, and remove both from shortening. To the same shortening add tomato purée, garlic and parsley, then mashed beans with their liquid, adding more water if it is too thick. Season, adding more salt if necessary, and let cook for 10 or 15 minutes.

To serve, add tortillas cut in small pieces, sausage and

grated cheese. In Mexico brown beans are used some times instead of the black. For 8 or 10.

SHRIMP SOUP

Prunes	6
Almonds	12
Shortening	3 tablespoons
Minced onion	2 tablespoons
Garlic	1 small clove (optional)
Peeled and seeded tomatoes	3
Stock	7 cups
Fresh or frozen shrimp	1 pound
Salt and pepper	To taste
Cream	1 cup
Chopped parsley	2 tablespoons

Soak prunes for several hours. Blanch almonds and fry until golden brown in half the shortening. In the same shortening fry onion and garlic. Put in liquidizer with chopped tomatoes, a little stock or water, and soft prunes (pitted). Fry the resulting pulp in the other half of the shortening, adding water or stock and raw shrimps cleaned and cut in small pieces. Season well with salt and pepper and boil until shrimps are cooked.

A little before serving add cream and chopped parsley. Serve very hot with fried croutons if desired. For 8.

SOUP CUAUHTEMOC   (*Sopa Cuauhtemoc*)

Dry tortillas	10
Large tomato	1
Fat	2 tablespoons
Minced onion	1 teaspoon
Garlic	1 clove (optional)
Parsley	2 tablespoons
Stock	2 quarts
Cooked spinach	1 cup
Salt and pepper	To taste
Grated cheese	To taste

It is advisable to make this soup the day after making enchiladas or any other dish that calls for tortillas, making ten extra ones and keeping them for the next day.

Chop the tomato, discarding the seeds. Fry in fat together with the onion, garlic and parsley. When very well fried, add strained stock and chopped spinach, and, last of all, small squares of the tortillas fried in butter. Serve with grated cheese. For 8.

CREAM OF AVOCADO SOUP

Butter	2 tablespoons
Flour	2 tablespoons
Milk	1 quart
Ripe avocados	2 (large)
Sweet cream	1 cup
Salt and pepper	To taste
Chili powder	To taste
Fried tortillas	3

Melt butter, add flour and mix until smooth. Remove

from fire and add hot milk little by little, stirring all the while. Return to slow fire and cook until mixture begins to thicken. Add one of the avocados mashed and passed through a sieve with a little lemon juice to prevent its getting dark. (If avocado is very smooth without strings, it is not necessary to put it through sieve.) Add the avocado pulp to cream sauce, together with cream. Season well and serve very hot accompanied by fried tortillas cut in small pieces, and the other avocado peeled and diced. For 4 or 6.

TAMALE SOUP

Breast of chicken	1
Tamales	6
Egg yolks	2
Cream	¼ cup
Salt	To taste

Mash the tamales or reduce to paste in liquidizer with a little of the stock. Pass through a sieve, adding more stock and egg yolks mixed with cream. Heat well, stirring constantly, and add the boiled breast of chicken cut in small pieces. Add salt if necessary and serve very hot. This is a very good way to serve leftover tamales. For 8.

Sauces

THERE ARE some international sauces used by all good cooks the world over. We use them profusely in Spain and Mexico. Cream Sauce, Béchamel, Mayonnaise are good old friends; but I am going to give the recipes of certain sauces that are less known and more typical.

ALMOND SAUCE SPANISH STYLE
(*Salsa de Almendra Española*)

Blanched almonds	½ cup
Hard-boiled egg yolks	2
Meat stock	2 cups
Salt and pepper	To taste

Toast blanched almonds and mash; mix with egg yolks.
Pass through sieve with stock and cook 15 or 20 minutes.
Season well and serve with meat or chicken. Makes 3 cups.

ALMOND SAUCE MEXICAN STYLE
(*Salsa de Almendra Mexicana*)

Fat	2 tablespoons
Blanched almonds	½ cup
Stale bread	1 slice
Tomatoes	2
Minced onion	1 teaspoon
Garlic	1 clove (optional)
Clove	1
Peppercorns	2
Salt and pepper	To taste
Stock	2 cups
Vinegar	2 tablespoons

Melt half of the fat and fry almonds and bread. Pass
through a fine food chopper together with tomatoes and
seasonings. Fry again in the rest of the fat and cook five
minutes. Add stock and vinegar. Cook until thick. Very
good with tongue. Makes 2½ cups.

POTATO SAUCE   (*Salsa de Papa*)

Large boiled potato	1
Hard-boiled egg yolks	2
Olive oil	3 tablespoons
Vinegar	1 teaspoon
Meat or fish stock	2 cups
Salt and pepper	To taste

Mash potato and egg yolks. Add olive oil, vinegar and stock and season well. Cook for a few minutes. Use meat stock when you are to serve the sauce with sliced, boiled meat and fish stock when it is to be served with fish. Makes 2 cups.

GIBLET SAUCE (*Salsa de Menudencias de Pollo*)

Tomatoes	2
Chicken or turkey giblets	Heart, liver and gizzard
Stale bread	1 slice
Minced onion	1 teaspoon
Minced garlic	1 clove
Parsley	1 teaspoon
Stock	2 cups
Salt and pepper	To taste

Peel tomatoes, cut in half, discard the seeds, and chop. Fry the giblets and bread, pass through fine food chopper together with onion, garlic, parsley and tomatoes and fry again. Add stock and season well. Cook until thick. Serve with chicken. Makes about 2½ cups.

RED SAUCE (*Salsa Roja*)

Large cooked beet	1
Cooked carrots	2
Minced onion	1 tablespoon
Butter	1 tablespoon
Flour	1 teaspoon
Stock	2 cups
Salt and pepper	To taste

Mash vegetables until reduced to a fine paste. Melt butter,

add flour, and when brown add paste, then stock. Season well with salt and pepper and cook for a few minutes. Serve with meat. Makes 2 cups.

ONION SAUCE (*Salsa de Cebolla*)

Large onions	2
Parsley	1 bunch
Bread, soaked in vinegar	1 slice
Stock or hot water	2 cups
Salt and pepper	To taste
Olive oil	3 tablespoons
Garlic cloves	2

Boil onions and mash with parsley and soaked bread. Pass through sieve with stock or water and season well.

Heat oil and brown garlic cloves. Remove these and add onion and parsley purée. Cook until the desired consistency. Makes 2 cups.

For the recipes that call for tomato sauce to be served apart from, or over, the meat, fish, etc., the following very simple sauce can be used.

TOMATO SAUCE (*Salsa de Tomate*)

Shortening	2 tablespoons
Minced onion	2 tablespoons
Minced garlic	1 teaspoon (optional)
Fresh or canned tomatoes or pulp	2 cups
Water or stock	1 cup
Small bay leaf	1
Minced parsley	1 tablespoon
Salt	To taste

Heat shortening, fry onion and garlic. Before it browns, add tomatoes and cook for a few minutes. Add water or stock, bay leaf, parsley and salt to taste. Cook until desired thickness is obtained. If tomato is too sour, one teaspoon of sugar may be added.

Rice

If CORN AND BEANS are the main food of the natives in Mexico, rice is certainly one of the foods which the middle-class people consume the most. It is served almost every day of the year in both the noon and evening meals. It is eaten as an entrée after soup and before the meat course.

Even if prepared very simply, it is delicious because its kernels stand separated and at the same time remain moist and rich.

In Spain, rice is also a favorite dish; the paella, or rice as the Valencians make it, is known the world over.

PLAIN WHITE RICE   (*Arroz Blanco*)

Rice   ½ pound
Shortening   3 tablespoons

Garlic	2 cloves (optional)
Onion	1
Hot water	1 quart
Salt	To taste
Parsley	1 sprig

Soak the rice in hot water for 15 minutes. Wash thoroughly with cold water until this comes out clear. Drain well. Melt the shortening and when it is hot add rice, garlic and onion, stirring constantly to keep from burning. When rice is transparent and begins to turn golden, add the quart of hot water, salt and parsley. Cover and cook gently over slow fire until rice is soft and each kernel stands apart (around 45 minutes). If it gets too dry and is not well done, more water may be added, but very little at a time.

This rice may be eaten alone or as an accompaniment to meat, chicken, eggs or any entree. Makes 3 cups.

WHITE RICE WITH FRIED BANANAS
(*Arroz Blanco con Plátanos Fritos*)

White rice	As first recipe
Bananas	3
Flour	½ cup
Shortening	½ cup

Choose very firm bananas. Peel, cut in slices lengthwise. Roll well in flour and fry in hot fat until golden brown. Serve them surrounding mound of rice. For 4 or 6.

CROWN OF RICE WITH AVOCADO SAUCE
(Corona de Arroz con Guacamole)

White rice	As first recipe
Butter	2 tablespoons
Avocados	3
Tomatoes (fresh or canned)	3
Minced onion	1 tablespoon
Minced parsley	1 tablespoon
Olive oil	2 tablespoons
Salt and chili sauce (or chili powder)	To taste

After making the white rice as in first recipe, pack well in buttered ring mold. Cover and place in pan of boiling water for 25 or 30 minutes.

Meanwhile peel avocados, chop or dice. Combine with chopped tomatoes, minced onion, parsley and olive oil. Season well with salt and if desired add chili sauce or powder. Leave one of the avocado seeds in mixture to prevent the avocado from turning black. (No fire is needed to make this sauce.) For 4 or 6.

Turn rice ring on hot round platter and put avocado sauce in the center.

RICE AND MEAT MOLD
(*Torta de Arroz con Picadillo*)

Rice	½ pound
Eggs, separated	3
Shortening	1 tablespoon
Ground pork	½ pound
Ground veal	½ pound
Sliced fresh tomatoes	1 cup
Almonds	18
Raisins	18
Butter	3 tablespoons

Wash the rice. Steam or boil with salt and drain. Beat the egg whites until stiff, add yolks one by one and continue beating. Mix them thoroughly with the rice.

Heat shortening, add ground meat, then tomatoes and skinned almonds and soaked raisins. Cook for a few minutes until quite dry.

Butter a plain mold, place layers of rice and layers of meat alternately, the last and first being of rice. Dot with butter and bake in hot oven.

Unmold on hot platter and dust with sugar and cinnamon. If this is not liked, serve with tomato sauce. For 4 or 6.

RICE WITH OKRA (*Arroz con Okra*)

Rice	½ pound
Olive oil	4 tablespoons
Minced onion	1 tablespoon
Minced garlic	1 clove (optional)
Okra	¼ pound
Ham	¼ pound
Tomato sauce	1 cup
Minced parsley	1 tablespoon
Salt	To taste
Hot stock or water	1 quart

Soak rice in hot water for 15 minutes, wash well in cold water, drain. Heat oil and add rice, onion and garlic; cook until brown, stirring constantly. Add sliced okra (without the heads) and chopped ham.

After a few minutes add tomato sauce, parsley and salt. Cook for five minutes and then add stock or water. Cover; cook gently until rice is done but not too dry. For 4 or 6.

RICE WITH FISH (*Arroz con Pescado*)

Red snapper, halibut or similar fish	½ pound
Rice	½ pound
Olive oil	½ cup
Chopped onion	1 tablespoon
Minced garlic	1 clove
Hot water or stock	1 quart
Saffron	1 pinch
Minced parsley	1 tablespoon
Salt	To taste
Hard-boiled egg	1
Red pimento	1

Clean fish, cut in pieces, sprinkle with salt and lemon juice and let stand for one hour.

Soak rice in hot water 15 minutes, wash with cold water and drain.

Heat oil; fry drained and wiped fish, put on platter or paper towel. In the same oil, fry onion, garlic and rice until golden brown, stirring constantly. Add hot water or stock, saffron, parsley and salt. Cover and cook gently. When rice is half done add fish and finish cooking.

Serve on hot platter garnished with slices of hard-boiled egg and strips of pimento. For 4 or 6.

RICE WITH CHICKEN (*Arroz con Pollo*)

Young tender chicken	1
Shortening	4 tablespoons
Onions	2
Garlic	1 clove (optional)
Tomatoes	2
Hot water	5 cups
Rice	½ pound
Peas	1 small can
Saffron	1 pinch
Salt and pepper	To taste
Red pimentos	2
Ripe olives	1 can

Clean and cut the chicken in small pieces. Fry in half of the shortening with the minced onion and garlic. When golden brown add the chopped tomatoes and after five minutes add 2 cups of the hot water. When chicken is almost done and nearly dry, add the rice previously washed and fried in another pan with the other half of the shortening. Mix well with the chicken, add the peas and the other

3 cups of hot water and the saffron. Cover and cook very gently until rice is done.

Serve on a hot platter garnished with the red pimentos cut in strips and the ripe olives. For 4 or 6.

RICE WITH SAUSAGES   (*Arroz con Salchichas*)

Water	5 cups
Garlic	1 clove
Onion	1
Bay leaf	1
Carrots	3
Sliced cabbage	1 cup
Salt	To taste
Shortening	3 tablespoons
Rice	½ pound
Peas	1 small can
Pork or Vienna sausages	8
Eggs	3
Grated cheese	3 tablespoons

Place on fire a pan with 5 cups of water with the garlic, half of the onion, the bay leaf, the carrots, cabbage and salt.

Heat shortening, add the other half of the onion minced and the washed rice (as usual). When golden brown add the vegetable stock with the sliced cabbage and the other vegetables cut in cubes. Add peas. Mix well, cover and cook gently. Meanwhile fry the sausages in a little shortening. Turn the almost dry and cooked rice into a buttered baking dish and place sausages on top. Beat the eggs lightly and pour over the rice. Put in oven to finish cooking and brown.

Before serving sprinkle the grated cheese over all. For 4 or 6.

RICE BARCELONA (*Arroz a la Catalána*)

Shortening	3 tablespoons
Onion	1
Garlic	1 clove (optional)
Chicken or	
rabbit meat, cut in pieces	2 cups
Tomato sauce	½ cup
Hot water	1 quart
Rice	½ pound
Paprika	1 teaspoon
Saffron	1 pinch
Clams	2 dozen
Peas	1 cup
Hearts of artichokes	4
Almonds	18
Pimentos	2
Parsley	1 sprig
Salt and pepper	To taste

Melt the shortening, add the minced onion and garlic, then the chicken or rabbit cut in small pieces. When brown, add tomato sauce and cook five minutes more, then hot water (two cups). Cook until meat is nearly tender and then add rice (fried in another pan), paprika, saffron and the other two cups of water (hot).

Heat the clams with a little water in another pan until shells open; clean clams and add to the boiling rice mixture with the peas and artichokes. Blanch and grind almonds with the red pimentos and a sprig of parsley and add to the rice. Should the rice get too dry a little more water may be added. For 4 or 6.

RICE VALENCIA STYLE (PAELLA)
(*Arroz a la Valenciana*)

Lard	3 tablespoons
Minced onion	1 tablespoon
Young chicken	½
Ham	¼ pound
Tomato sauce	1 cup
Stock or hot water	5 cups
Olive oil	3 tablespoons
Garlic	1 clove
Fish	3 slices
Rice	¾ pound
Shrimps	1 dozen
Minced parsley	1 tablespoon
Saffron	1 pinch
Salt	To taste
Sausages	6
Hearts of artichokes	6
Red pimentos	2

Melt the lard in a pan, add the minced onion and the chicken cut in small pieces, the raw ham cut in small cubes. When brown add the tomato sauce and cook five minutes, then add three cups of stock or water, cover and cook gently. In another pan heat oil with garlic. When the clove is brown take it out and fry fish slices. Take them out and keep on warm platter. In the same oil fry rice until light golden brown and add together with the oil to the pan where the chicken is boiling; add shrimps (cleaned), parsley, saffron and salt to taste. Add remaining two cups of stock or hot water, cover and cook gently. When rice is half done, add sausages, fish cut in pieces and hearts of artichoke. Cover and let cook until rice is done but not too dry. Add more water if necessary. Serve very hot in the same container. Garnish with pimentos cut in strips. For 6 or 8.

RICE WITH CHICKEN LIVERS OR LAMB KIDNEYS
(*Arroz con Hígaditos de Pollo*)

White rice	As in first recipe of this section
Livers or kidneys	10
Onion	1 cup
Shortening	2 tablespoons
Ham	¼ pound
Tomato sauce	1 cup
Sherry wine	½ cup
Stock	1 quart
Salt	To taste

Put rice in buttered mold and place in pan of boiling water for 25 or 30 minutes.

Chop, coarsely, the chicken livers or the kidneys and fry with minced onion in the hot shortening. When slightly brown add cubed ham and tomato sauce. Cook five minutes, add wine and stock. Cook gently until meats are tender.

Turn rice mold onto hot platter and pour the sauce over it. For 4 or 6.

RICE WITH GREEN PEPPERS AND CHEESE
(*Arroz con Chiles Poblanos y Queso*)

Rice	¾ pound
Small green peppers	8
Grated Parmesan cheese	¼ pound
Cream	1 pint
Salt and pepper	To taste
Butter	2 tablespoons

Prepare the rice as in first recipe of this section. Boil the peppers 15 minutes. Drain and stuff with half of the cheese.

Butter a baking dish and place in it a layer of rice; arrange the stuffed peppers and half of the cream and some cheese. Another layer of rice, the rest of the cream and cheese. Dot with butter and put in hot oven to brown. For 8.

PICNIC RICE

Long-grained rice	½ pound
Cooking oil	3 tablespoons
Olive oil	2 tablespoons
Onion	1
Garlic	1 clove
Chicken broth	5 cups
English mustard	1 tablespoon
Parsley	1 sprig
Salt	To taste
Grated cheese	½ cup

Soak rice in hot water for 15 minutes. Wash in cold water until water comes out clear. Drain well and fry in hot oil with the whole onion and whole garlic clove, until it begins to get light yellow; it should not get brown. Drain excess oil and add hot chicken broth with mustard, parsley and salt. Cover and cook over slow fire until soft and dry. Place in casserole or deep serving dish and, while hot, sprinkle generously with grated cheese.

Discard onion and garlic clove before serving. For 8 or 10.

BLACK RICE

Raw black beans	¼ cup
Cooking oil	2 tablespoons
Onion	1
Salt	To taste
Rice	½ pound
Oil	3 tablespoons
Garlic	1 clove
Onion	1 small
Tomato paste or purée	3 tablespoons
Bean liquid	5 cups
Salt	To taste
Parsley	1 sprig
Diced boiled ham	½ cup
Peas	1 small can
Artichoke hearts	6 (optional)
Grated cheese	To taste

To make bean liquid: Soak beans overnight. Next morning boil beans with plenty of water with oil, whole onion and salt until soft. (This can be done in pressure cooker.) When lukewarm put the beans in liquidizer with 5 cups of their liquor. Mixture should not be thick.

Soak rice in hot water for 15 minutes, wash well with cold water and drain. Fry in hot oil with garlic and another small onion. When light brown add tomato purée, fry one or two minutes longer and add bean liquid, salt and parsley sprig. Cover and let cook on slow fire.

When half done add diced ham, canned peas and boiled artichoke hearts.

To serve, sprinkle with grated cheese. For 10 or 12.

The entrees of macaroni, rice, etc., have, in Mexico, a peculiar name — *Sopa seca* — that means dry soup. Here are some:

BREAD DRY SOUP   (*Sopa Seca de Pan*)

Stale rolls	6
Shortening	6 tablespoons
Minced garlic	1 clove (optional)
Minced onion	1 teaspoon
Tomato sauce	1 cup
Minced parsley	1 teaspoon
Hot stock	1 quart
Salt and pepper	To taste
Boiled sliced carrots	6
Grated cheese	3 tablespoons

Slice the rolls and toast the slices. Melt shortening and fry 6 of the slices. Set them aside. In the same fat fry minced garlic and onion; when these are transparent add tomato sauce and parsley. Cook five minutes, then add hot stock. Cook five minutes longer.

Butter a baking dish and place alternate layers of toasted bread, carrots and cheese, putting the fried slices of bread on top. Pour the sauce over all (bread should be soaked), sprinkle with cheese and bake in hot oven to brown. For 6.

TOTOPOS DRY SOUP   (*Sopa Seca de Tortillas*)

Small tortillas	24
Shortening	2 tablespoons
Large onion	1
Cream cheese	1 package
Cream	1 pint
Green pepper	1
Salt and pepper	To taste

Make tortillas as for enchiladas. Melt shortening and fry lightly each tortilla but without allowing them to get brown or dry. In the same fat, cook the sliced onion until transparent. Cut cream cheese in cubes. On each fried tortilla put a little of the cream cheese and one or two slices of onion. Roll and place in buttered baking dish. Whip the cream and arrange alternate layers of rolled tortillas, cream, and bits of cheese. On top of everything put strips of green pepper, cream and cheese. Bake in the oven 20 or 25 minutes. For 8.

MACARONI WITH CHILE CON CARNE
(*Macarrones con Chile con Carne*)

Boiled macaroni	½ pound
Butter	½ cup
Grated cheese	1 cup
Chili con carne	1 can

Heat boiled macaroni in half of the butter. Butter baking dish and arrange alternate layers of macaroni, cheese, and chili con carne. The last one should be macaroni with cheese and bits of butter.

Bake in oven until brown. For 6 or 8.

NOODLES WITH HOT SAUCE
(*Tallarínes con Salsa Picante*)

Noodles	½ pound
Onion	1 whole
Butter	¼ cup
Salt	To taste
Minced onion	1 teaspoon
Tomato sauce	2 cups
Minced parsley	1 teaspoon
Red chili powder	1 tablespoon
Vienna sausages	1 can
Grated cheese	1 cup

Boil noodles with one whole onion in plenty of salted water. When done place under running water and drain. Heat in half of the melted butter. Season with salt.

Heat the other half of the butter and fry minced onion; when soft, add tomato sauce, parsley and chili powder. Cook five minutes. Add sliced sausage.

Butter a baking dish and place alternate layers of noodles, sauce and sausage, and grated cheese. Place noodles on top with grated·cheese and bits of butter. Bake in oven until brown. For 6 or 8.

PANCAKES WITH CHICKEN   (*Crepas con Pollo*)
BATTER

Flour	½ cup
Salt	½ teaspoon
Milk	½ cup
Cooking oil	2 tablespoons
Eggs	3

Place flour sifted with salt in a bowl, add milk little by

little and beat until smooth; add oil and beaten eggs. The batter should be creamy and smooth. For the first pancake, rub a little butter in a small frying pan. Make pancakes thin. Keep warm over hot water.

Cooked breast of chicken	1
Fried tomato sauce	1 cup
Cream	1 cup
Grated cheese	1 cup
Salt and pepper	To taste

Shred chicken and mix with fried tomato sauce. Butter baking dish and place alternate layers of pancakes, chicken, cream and grated cheese. The last layer should be of pancakes, cream and cheese. Bake in oven until brown. For 8.

PANCAKES WITH GREEN PEPPERS
(*Crepas con Chile Poblano*)

Pancakes	As in above recipe
Cream	1 pint
Green peppers	2
Grated cheese	1 cup
Salt	To taste

Make pancakes as in previous recipe. Butter a baking dish and put in it alternate layers of pancakes, cream, green pepper strips (seeded and boiled ten minutes) and grated cheese. Bake in oven until brown. For 6 or 8.

XOCHITL PUDDING (*Budín Xochitl*)

White cornmeal	3 cups
Milk	1 pint
Salt	To taste
Butter	½ cup
Grated cheese	¼ pound
Sauce	2 cups

Put cornmeal, milk and salt in saucepan. Cook over slow fire, stirring constantly until very thick (like a dough). Roll this dough about ⅓ inch thick. Cool and cut in small squares.

In a buttered baking dish put alternate layers of the dough squares, bits of butter, grated cheese and a little of the sauce. Bake 20 minutes in hot oven.

SAUCE

Bacon	¼ pound
Beef (ground)	1 pound
Onion	1
Carrots	2
Tomato soup	1 can
Bay leaf	1
Marjoram	1 pinch
Salt	To taste
Water	2 cups

Put bacon in frying pan. When fat is melted, add meat. Brown well and remove to a saucepan.

To fat in frying pan add sliced onion and carrots. Cook until onion is soft, then add tomato soup, herbs and salt. Cook for 5 minutes and add water. Add this to the meat, cover and cook on slow fire until meat is tender. If necessary, add more water. There should be two cups of the sauce. For 8 or 10.

Eggs

MEXICAN TIMBALES (Cold)

Minced parsley	3 tablespoons
Eggs	6
Butter	2 tablespoons
Salt and pepper	To taste
Thick tomato slices	6
French dressing	6 tablespoons

Butter small timbale molds or custard cups and sprinkle well with the chopped parsley. Break a whole egg in each. Dot with butter, salt and pepper. Place in a pan with hot water up to ½ of the molds. Put over fire or in oven until eggs are set.

Put slices of tomato on individual salad plates and pour over each 1 tablespoon of French dressing. Turn an egg timbale on each. Serve as entree or salad.

The colors are red, white and green — the colors of the Mexican flag. For 6.

MEXICAN TIMBALES (Hot)

Prepare eggs as in above recipe, but in place of the cold tomato use six slices of fried, toasted bread, cover with hot tomato sauce, and place the egg timbales on them.

EGGS RANCH STYLE   (*Huevos Rancheros*)

Tortillas	6
Shortening	½ cup
Minced onion	1 tablespoon
Flour	1 teaspoon
Tomato sauce	2 cups
Minced parsley	1 tablespoon
Red chili powder	1 teaspoon
Green pepper	1 (optional)
Salt and pepper	To taste
Eggs	6

Make half of the recipe given for Tortillas. Allow to dry a few hours. Near serving time, fry them in hot fat and drain on paper towel.

Put a little of the fat in another saucepan and add onion; when it is transparent add flour to brown, then tomato sauce and parsley, also chili powder and green pepper, if desired. Season well with salt.

Place tortillas on hot platter, put a fried egg on each and

cover with the hot sauce. Serve immediately. Grated cheese may be sprinkled on top. For 6.

MEXICAN SCRAMBLED EGGS (*Huevos Revueltos*)

Eggs	6
Fat	3 tablespoons
Minced onion	1 teaspoon
Minced parsley	1 teaspoon
Large tomato	1
Chili sauce or powder	1 teaspoon
Salt	To taste

Beat eggs as for omelet. Melt fat and add onion. When transparent add parsley, chopped tomato and chili sauce or powder. Cook two or three minutes and add eggs, stirring constantly until cooked but tender. These eggs may be served on toast or in the center of a crown of rice. For 6.

EGGS CHAPULTEPEC (*Huevos Chapultepec*)

Processed cheese	6 slices
Boiled diced tongue	½ cup
Minced pickles	2 tablespoons
Eggs	6
Catsup	6 tablespoons
Chili sauce	3 teaspoons
Salt	To taste
Butter	2 tablespoons

Butter a baking dish and place in it slices of cream cheese, diced tongue and minced pickles. Break eggs onto this layer. On top of each egg place a tablespoon of catsup mixed with half a teaspoon of chili sauce. Salt and dot with butter. Bake in oven until whites are set but yolks soft. For 6.

EGGS SAN LUIS POTOSI STYLE (*Huevos Potosinos*)

Green pepper	1
Butter or other shortening	2 tablespoons
Minced onion	1 teaspoon
Tomato soup	1 can
Soda	1 pinch
Scalded milk	1 cup
Processed cheese	6 slices
Cream	1 cup
Hard-boiled eggs	6
Salt	To taste
Minced parsley	1 teaspoon

Boil green pepper for ten minutes. Seed and cut in strips. Melt shortening; add onion and when transparent add tomato soup, soda, then milk, cheese, cream and hard-boiled eggs (sliced). Add parsley. Keep in double boiler until serving time. For 6 or 8.

Serve on fried tortillas or toast.

EGGS WITH GREEN SAUCE (*Huevos en Salsa Verde*)

Eggs	6
Minced onion	1 teaspoon
Minced parsley	1 tablespoon
Minced olives	3 tablespoons
Minced capers	1 tablespoon
Salt and pepper	To taste
Butter	2 tablespoons
Pea soup	1 can

Hard-boil eggs. Cut in halves lengthwise and take out yolks, mash and mix with onion, parsley, olives and capers. Season well with salt and pepper. Melt one tablespoon of the butter and fry mixture. When very thick, refill the egg whites (they will have to be overstuffed). Place them on hot platter.

Melt the rest of the butter and add canned pea soup. Cook a few minutes and cover the egg halves. For 6.

EGGS IN TOMATO SAUCE WITH CHEESE
(*Huevos en Salsa de Tomate con Queso*)

Green pepper	1
Fat	2 tablespoons
Minced onion	1 tablespoon
Tomato sauce	3 cups
Parsley	1 tablespoon
Chili powder	1 teaspoon
Salt	To taste
Eggs	6
Processed cheese	6 slices

Boil green pepper, seed it and cut in strips. Melt fat, add onion, and when transparent, add tomato sauce, parsley and chili powder. Cook five minutes. Add green pepper strips.

Near serving time, heat sauce and when it begins to boil, break eggs into it gently, one by one; add cheese slices. Serve immediately. Egg yolks should be soft. For 6.

FISH WITH PARSLEY SAUCE
(*Pescado con Salsa de Perejil*)

Parsley	1 bunch
Garlic	1 small clove
Minced onion	1 teaspoon
Butter	½ cup
White wine	2 cups
Salt and pepper	To taste
Halibut or similar fish	2 pounds

Pass through food chopper parsley, garlic and onion. Fry in the butter and add the wine. Season with salt and pepper.

Wash fish and rub with lemon, salt and pepper. Put in

baking pan, pour the sauce, cover fish and bake in moderate oven. For 4 or 6.

SPANISH FISH   (*Pescado a la Española*)

Fish fillets	8
Bay leaf	1
Lemon	1 slice
Olive oil	¼ cup
Tomatoes	6
Garlic	1 clove
Minced onion	1 tablespoon
Salt and pepper	To taste
Almonds	10
Raisins	15
Capers	1 tablespoon
Vinegar	1 tablespoon

Clean the fillets and simmer in water with some salt, 1 bay leaf and one lemon slice for 6 minutes.

Heat the oil and fry the chopped tomatoes, minced garlic and onion. Add 1 cup of the fish stock, salt and pepper. Add the fillets and the blanched and halved almonds, raisins (previously soaked in water) and capers. Finally add the vinegar and serve very hot. For 8.

FISH WITH ORANGE SAUCE
(*Pescado en Salsa de Naranja*)

Fish slices	8
Lemon	1
Salt and pepper	To taste
Olive oil	¼ cup
Tomatoes	2
Onion	1
Oranges	4
Stuffed olives	18
Gherkins	12

Wash the fish and let stand for one hour in lemon juice, salt and pepper. Put half of the oil in baking pan. Lay the fish on it. Place over it chopped tomatoes, minced onion and the remaining oil.

Bake in moderate oven. When fish begins to brown, add the juice of two oranges. Serve on a hot platter with strained sauce over it. Garnish with stuffed olives, orange slices (or sections) and gherkins. For 8.

FISH IN TOMATO SAUCE
(*Pescado en Salsa de Tomate Rojo*)

Melted butter	¼ cup
Olive oil	¼ cup
Minced onion	1 tablespoon
Minced garlic	1 clove (optional)
Tomato sauce	2 cups
Minced parsley	1 tablespoon
Whole fish	2 pounds
Sherry wine	½ cup

Heat butter and oil; add onion and garlic and when transparent add tomato and parsley. Cook 5 minutes, then add fish and wine.

Season well and simmer gently. Turn fish just once. Garnish with olives. For 4 or 6.

DE LUXE SPANISH FISH
(*Pescado de Lujo a la Española*)

Whole fish	1½ pounds
Onion	1
Bay leaf	1
Salt and pepper	To taste
Tomato sauce	2 cups
Shortening	1 tablespoon
Oysters	1 can
Shrimps	1 can
Stuffed olives	12
Peas	½ cup
Boiled and diced carrots	½ cup
Brandy	1 liqueur glass
Sherry wine	½ cup
Cornstarch	1 tablespoon

Clean the fish and place in a pan with a little water, the onion, bay leaf and salt. Simmer for a few minutes. Drain, removing the bay leaf and onion. Cover fish with the tomato sauce (which has been fried in the shortening), add the oysters with their water, the chopped shrimps, olives, boiled peas, carrots, brandy and sherry, the cornstarch diluted in a little water, and cook until the fish is tender but not mushy. For 4.

FISH WITH HOT SAUCE, VERACRUZ STYLE
(*Pescado a la Veracruzana*)

Olive oil	½ cup
Minced onion	1 teaspoon
Minced garlic	1 clove
Tomato sauce	2 cups
Ground peppercorns	2
Ground cinnamon	⅛ teaspoon
Ground cloves	2
Red chili powder	2 tablespoons
Sugar	½ teaspoon
Fish fillets or slices	8
Potatoes	3
Olives	18
Bread slices	4
Lemon slices	½ lemon

Heat half of the olive oil and fry onion and garlic. When transparent, add tomato sauce, spices and chili powder. When well fried, add sugar and a little water, if too thick.

Heat the remaining oil and fry fish. Add to the sauce with boiled and cubed potatoes. Garnish with olives and with triangles of bread, fried in butter and lemon slices.

If not wanted very sharp, use one tablespoon of chili powder instead of two. For 8.

FISH WITH CAPER SAUCE
(*Pescado con Salsa de Alcaparras*)

Fish fillets	8
Onion	1
Bay leaf	1
Salt and pepper	To taste
Butter	½ cup
Flour	2 tablespoons
Capers	½ cup

Simmer fillets in a little water with sliced onion, one bay leaf and salt.

Melt butter, add flour and when light brown add the water in which the fish was boiled (about 1½ cups). Cook for a few minutes.

Add capers and pour over the fillets. Serve very hot. For 8.

CAMPECHE FRIED FISH
(*Pescado Frito a la Campechana*)

Fish fillets or slices	6
Flour	6 tablespoons
Shortening	½ cup

Dip fillets in flour and fry in hot shortening. Cover with hot sauce.

SAUCE

Large onion	1
Vinegar	½ cup
Water	½ cup
Oregano	To taste
Salt	To taste

Boil sliced onion with vinegar, water and oregano until onion is transparent. For 6.

FISH WITH OLIVE SAUCE
(*Pescado con Salsa de Aceitunas*)

Fish fillets	8
Salt and pepper	To taste
Minced parsley	1 tablespoon
Lemon	1
Dry bread crumbs	1 cup
Raw eggs	2

Wash fillets, sprinkle with salt, pepper and parsley. Pour lemon juice over them and place in icebox.

Shortly before serving dip in bread crumbs, then in beaten eggs and again in bread crumbs. Fry gently in deep fat. Keep warm.

SAUCE

Large pimento-stuffed olives	6
Garlic	1 clove (optional)
Onion	½
Parsley	1 small bunch
Olive oil	6 tablespoons
Hard-boiled eggs	3
Tomato juice	½ cup
Mustard	1 teaspoon
Salt	To taste

Pass olives, garlic, onion and parsley through fine food chopper. Mix with olive oil, mashed egg yolks, tomato juice and mustard. Season well with salt. Serve cold with hot fish. For 8.

STUFFED FISH (No. 1) (*Pescado Relleno*)

Whole fish	2 pounds
Tomatoes	One No. 2 can
Potatoes	3
Almonds	10
Capers	10
Lard	1 tablespoon
Minced onion	1 tablespoon
Vinegar	1 teaspoon
Sugar	1 teaspoon
Salt and pepper	To taste
Olive oil	3 tablespoons
Lemon	1
Minced parsley	1 teaspoon

Select almost any fish such as weakfish or a small haddock. Slit nearly the whole length of the fish.

Chop tomatoes, boiled potatoes, almonds and capers.

Melt shortening and add onion and all the chopped ingredients except parsley. Add vinegar, sugar, salt and pepper to taste. Cook until quite dry. Brush fish inside with oil and salt. Stuff. Skewer. Place in baking pan and cover with the remaining oil and the juice of the lemon.

When done, sprinkle with the parsley and serve hot. For 4 or 6.

STUFFED FISH (No. 2) (*Pescado Relleno*)

Whole fish	2 pounds
Lemons	2
Lard	1 tablespoon
Olive oil	½ cup
Minced onion	1 tablespoon
Tomatoes	1 large can
Minced parsley	1 tablespoon
Dry bread crumbs	½ cup
Peas	1 small can
Cauliflower	1
Salt and pepper	To taste
Red pimentos	2

Clean fish. Slit nearly the whole length and let stand in lemon juice for a few hours.

Melt fat and add a little of the oil. When hot, add onion; when transparent, add chopped tomatoes and parsley and cook 5 minutes. Add bread crumbs, peas, and half of the boiled cauliflower divided in small pieces. Stuff fish. Season well with salt and pepper.

Oil a baking pan, place fish on it and cover with oil. Bake about 20 minutes. Transfer to hot platter, garnish with cauliflower portions and strips of pimento. For 4 or 6.

FISH POTPOURRI

Fish	2 pounds
Onions	1 pound
Tomatoes	6
Paprika or chili powder	1 teaspoon
Salt	To taste
Red pimentos	2
Sherry wine	1 cup
Oil	½ cup

Select two or three kinds of fish: fresh cod, halibut or any other kind. Clean and cut in pieces. Butter a baking dish and alternate layers of fish, sliced onion, sliced tomatoes, paprika or chili powder and salt. Garnish the top with pimento strips and pour wine and oil over all. Bake in 325° oven for 30 minutes. For 6 or 8.

FISH WITH OYSTERS (*Pescado con Ostiones*)

Olive oil	½ cup
Sliced onions	¼ pound
Tomatoes	1 can
Salt, pepper and paprika	To taste
Flaked fish	2 pounds
Peas	1 cup
Oysters	18
Red pimentos	2
Dry bread crumbs	

Heat half of the oil. Add onion and when it is transparent add chopped tomatoes, salt and pepper. Cook ten minutes. Add fish and peas. Cook ten minutes longer, mixing well. Transfer to a baking dish, placing oysters and strips of pimento on top, then bread crumbs and remaining oil. Brown in the oven. For 6 or 8.

STUFFED CABBAGE WITH OYSTERS
(*Col Rellena con Ostiones*)

Cabbage	1
Shortening	2 tablespoons
Minced onion	1 tablespoon
Garlic	1 clove (optional)
Tomatoes	1 small can
Salt and pepper	To taste
Vinegar	1 teaspoon
Sugar	1 teaspoon
Oysters	12
Parsley, minced	¼ cup
Pimento-stuffed olives	10
Capers	15

Parboil cabbage in salted water. Make a hollow in the center. Prepare stuffing as follows:

Melt shortening. Add minced onion and garlic. When transparent, add tomatoes, salt, pepper, vinegar and sugar. Cook ten minutes; add oysters, parsley, olives and capers. Cook until quite dry.

Stuff cabbage. Cover hollow with some cabbage leaves and tie with a string. Pour some olive oil or melted butter on the cabbage and bake at 350° for about 45 minutes. For 4 or 6.

Serve hot with Béchamel or tomato sauce.

SPANISH OYSTERS   (*Ostiones a la Española*)

Butter	¼ cup
Chopped chives (or onion)	1 teaspoon
Flour	1 tablespoon
Stock	¼ cup
Sherry wine	¼ cup
Egg yolks	3
Fresh oysters	36
Salt and pepper	To taste
Dry bread crumbs	3 tablespoons

Melt the butter, fry chives (or onion), add the flour and brown. Add the stock and wine. Cook until thick. Remove from fire and add the beaten egg yolks, mixing well. Take the oysters from the shell and put them in the sauce. Place each with some sauce on a clean shell, sprinkle with crumbs and bake in hot oven until brown. For 6.

OYSTERS VERACRUZ STYLE
(*Ostiones a la Veracruzana*)

Large oysters	3 dozen
Salt and pepper	To taste
Lemons	2
Caraway seed or cumin seeds	¼ teaspoon
Lard or oil	2 tablespoons
Chopped onion	1 tablespoon
Chopped tomato	2 cups
Minced parsley	1 tablespoon
Eggs	4
Dry bread crumbs	½ cup
Butter	2 tablespoons

Drain oysters and let stand with salt and lemon juice. Mix pepper with crumbs and caraway seeds.

Heat lard or oil and add onion. When transparent add chopped tomato and parsley.

Beat egg whites until stiff. Add yolks one by one, beating constantly.

Butter deep dish and put in alternate layers of oysters, fried tomato mixture, egg mixture and bread crumbs. The last layer should be of bread crumbs. Dot with butter and bake in oven until brown. For 6.

SPICED SHRIMPS (*Camarones en Escabeche*)

Shortening	3 tablespoons
Flour	1 tablespoon
Minced onion	1 tablespoon
Minced garlic	1 clove
Ground peppercorns	3
Ground clove	1
Ground caraway or cumin seeds	⅛ teaspoon
Red chili powder	1 tablespoon
Minced parsley	1 tablespoon
Cleaned fresh shrimps	1 pound
Potatoes (boiled)	3
Salt and pepper	To taste

Heat shortening, add flour and when smooth add onion and garlic. When transparent add tomato sauce, spices and chili powder. Cook five minutes, add parsley, shrimps and boiled potatoes cut in cubes. Salt to taste. For 6 or 8.

MEXICAN CRABS (*Jaibas a la Mexicana*)

Olive oil	3 tablespoons
Minced onion	1 tablespoon
Tomatoes	1 small can
Red pimento	1
Olives	10
Almonds	10
Capers	18
Crabmeat	2 pounds
Dry bread crumbs	½ cup
Paprika or red chili powder	1 teaspoon
Salt and pepper	To taste
Hard-boiled eggs	2
Butter	2 tablespoons

Heat oil, fry onion until brown, add chopped tomatoes. Cook 5 minutes, then add chopped pimento, chopped olives, chopped blanched almonds, capers, crabmeat and half of the bread crumbs. Cook and season well with chili powder and salt. Take from fire; add chopped hard-boiled eggs. Fill crab shells with the mixture, sprinkle with more crumbs, dot with butter and brown in the oven. For 6 or 8.

FISH MOLD   (*Molde de Pescado*)

Cooked flaked fish	4 cups
Soda crackers	8
Red pimentos	3
Tomato sauce	1 cup
Eggs	8
Salt and pepper	To taste

Lettuce, mayonnaise, shrimps, and boiled beet

Mix flaked fish with ground crackers, chopped pimentos, the tomato sauce (fried previously in a little butter) and the yolks of the eggs. Beat egg whites until stiff and add to mixture. Season with salt and pepper and pour in greased mold. Bake at 350° in a pan of water until set.

When cold, serve garnished with lettuce, mayonnaise, diced beet and whole shrimps. For 4 or 6.

FISH RING   (*Corona de Pescado*)

White-meated fish	2 pounds
Eggs	4
Dry bread crumbs	½ cup
Minced onion	1 tablespoon
Minced parsley	1 tablespoon
Butter	½ cup

Lettuce, pimentos, hard-boiled eggs for garnish

Clean, boil and flake fish. Mix with the eggs, half of the bread crumbs, onion and parsley. Butter and sprinkle a ring mold with bread crumbs. Fill with mixture and more bread crumbs, then melted butter. Bake in oven, turn out on platter. Garnish with lettuce, hard-boiled eggs and pimentos. For 6 or 8.

FISH BALLS (*Albóndigas de Pescado*)

Oil	½ cup
Minced onion	1 tablespoon
Minced parsley	1 tablespoon
Leftover fish	2 cups
Raw eggs	2
Bread crumbs	¼ cup
Flour	3 tablespoons

Heat a little of the oil; add onion and parsley and cook until golden brown. Add to the minced fish. Add the slightly beaten raw eggs and the bread crumbs. Make balls and roll in flour. Fry in hot oil. Serve accompanied by tomato sauce to which one teaspoon of chili sauce or powder has been added, or use as a hot hors d'oeuvre, using the sauce as a dip. Makes 18 to 24 small balls.

POTATO AND FISH TURNOVERS
(*Empanadas de Pescado y Papa*)

Finely minced onion	1 tablespoon
Butter	1 tablespoon
Large boiled potatoes	4
Flour	¼ cup
Eggs	4
Parsley	1 teaspoon
Salt and pepper	To taste
Nutmeg	Pinch
Cooked fish	½ cup

Fry the minced onion in the butter; when cold add the mashed potatoes, flour, beaten eggs, parsley, salt, pepper and nutmeg. Roll and divide into small squares. Put in each a small portion of the leftover fish. Fold, pressing edges with fingers, and fry in deep hot fat.

Serve accompanied with tomato sauce or with a salad. For 8.

Dried cod is one of the most popular dishes in Spain and is served in endless ways.

DRIED COD WITH MILK (*Bacalao con Leche*)

Dried cod	1 pound
Potatoes	1 pound
Flour	½ cup
Olive oil	½ cup
Minced onion	2 tablespoons
Hot milk	1 cup
Hot water	1 cup
Salt and pepper	To taste
Minced parsley	2 tablespoons

Soak cod, changing water several times. Parboil. Drain, saving water. Clean, bone, and cut in pieces.

Boil and slice potatoes. Roll cod pieces in flour and fry in hot oil. In the remaining oil, fry onion until tender and add milk and one cup of the water in which the cod was boiled. Season with salt and pepper.

In a baking dish place alternate layers of fish, potatoes, parsley and milk sauce. Cover and bake in slow oven about 30 minutes. For 4 or 6.

DRIED COD VISCAY (*Bacalao a la Vizcaina*)

Boned dried cod	2 pounds
Soda	½ teaspoon
Minced onion	1 tablespoon
Olive oil	1 cup
Garlic	2 cloves
Thick tomato sauce	3 cups
Potatoes	½ pound
Red chili powder	2 tablespoons (optional)
Dry sherry wine	1 cup
Vinegar	2 tablespoons
Hot water	½ cup
Salt and pepper	To taste
Minced parsley	1 tablespoon
Olives	12
Red pimentos	2
Bread triangles fried in butter	12

Wash cod and soak overnight with ½ teaspoon of soda.

Next day wash thoroughly and put in saucepan with minced onion and water to cover. Heat well but do not boil.

Heat oil with whole garlic cloves. When these are brown, add tomato sauce and chili powder. Cook five minutes, then add cod, potatoes, wine, vinegar and ½ cup of the water in which cod was heated. Salt and pepper to taste. When cod and potatoes are done take out garlic cloves. Serve very hot garnished with parsley, olives, pimento strips and fried triangles of bread. For 6 or 8.

FISH MEXICAN FLAG

Whole fish — snook, red snapper or similar kind	3 pounds
Onion	1
Lemon	1 slice
Bay leaf, thyme and marjoram	1 pinch each
Salt and pepper	To taste
Almonds	¼ pound
Sesame seeds	2 tablespoons
Bread	2 slices
Water	¼ cup
Vinegar	1 tablespoon
Shortening	2 tablespoons
Olive oil	2 tablespoons
Sugar	1 teaspoon (optional)

Pomegranate seeds or red pimento for garnish

Boil fish with sliced onion, lemon slice, herbs and salt and pepper, being careful to keep whole.

Blanch almonds, toast sesame seeds until light brown and soak bread in water and vinegar. Reduce all this to paste in mortar, or in liquidizer, adding more water. Season with salt and pepper.

Heat shortening and fry paste. Remove from fire and add olive oil, sugar, if desired, and more vinegar if necessary.

Place whole fish on platter, taking skin off. When cold, cover with cold sauce. Garnish with watercress around fish and pomegranate seeds or pimento strips on top. For 6 or 8.

The Mexican flag is red, white and green — thus the name.

FISH WITH AVOCADO SAUCE

Whole fish	About 3 pounds
Avocados	3
Fresh or canned tomatoes	2
Minced onion	2 tablespoons
Minced parsley	2 tablespoons
Chili powder	To taste
Salt	To taste
Olives	12
Boiled or pickled small onions	24

Boil or bake fish as in previous recipes, keeping whole. Lift from pan carefully and skin while hot, transferring to platter in which it is going to be served.

Shortly before serving, peel and mash or dice avocados, peel, seed and chop tomatoes and mix both with minced onion, minced parsley, chili powder and salt. Cover fish, garnish with olives and onions. In Mexico, fresh coriander leaves are used instead of parsley, but it is a taste that has to be acquired and parsley suits foreign palates better.

If sauce is made in advance, salt should not be added until the last minute to avoid the darkening of the avocado. For 6 or 8.

FRIED FISH WITH AVOCADO SAUCE

Fish slices	8
Flour	½ cup
Salt and pepper	To taste
Shortening	½ cup
Garlic cloves	3
Avocado sauce	As in previous recipe

Wash and dry fish slices. Cover evenly with flour, salt and pepper.

Heat shortening and fry whole garlic cloves until dark brown. Remove and fry fish until well cooked and golden on both sides. Place on paper towel to remove excess grease, and serve at once with avocado sauce. For 4.

FISH WITH CHILI AND RED WINE SAUCE

Garlic	1 clove
Cumin seeds	½ teaspoon
Chili powder	2 teaspoons
Shortening	3 tablespoons
Fish slices or fillets	12
Green pepper	1
Tomatoes fresh or canned	3
Red wine	1 cup
Salt	To taste
Olive oil	3 tablespoons
Oregano	½ teaspoon
Minced parsley	2 tablespoons
Olives	12
Capers	24

Mash in mortar: garlic clove, cumin seeds and chili powder. Heat shortening and fry fish lightly, removing when it starts to get brown. In remaining shortening fry chopped green pepper, then paste of garlic, and lastly chopped tomatoes. Let cook for five minutes and add red wine, leaving for another minute. Season with salt.

In ovenproof dish place layers of fish, tomato and wine sauce, olive oil, dried oregano, minced parsley, olives and capers. Last layer should be of sauce and olive oil. Let stand for some time (or even overnight in the refrigerator, covered with aluminum foil).

Shortly before serving, heat well in 350° oven and serve at once. For 6 or 8.

BASS IN PAPER

Whole bass	2 pounds
Lemon, salt and pepper	To taste
Minced onion	2 tablespoons
Minced parsley	3 tablespoons
Dry bread crumbs	1 cup
Olive oil	4 tablespoons
Garlic	1 clove

Wash fish and make some gashes on the surface. Rub with lemon, salt and pepper, and sprinkle with minced onion, minced parsley and bread crumbs.

Wrap in brown heavy paper soaked in oil mixed with mashed garlic clove, and broil until done on grill, or in the oven over a grill with pan underneath to catch drippings.

Remove from paper and serve with the following sauce:

Hard-boiled eggs	3
Mustard	1 teaspoon
Salt and pepper	To taste
Oil	6 tablespoons
Vinegar	3 tablespoons
Large olives	6

Mash egg yolks, adding mustard, salt and pepper. Little by little add oil and vinegar and lastly chopped egg whites and chopped olives. Sauce should be served cold with hot fish.

Chili powder or Tabasco sauce to taste may be used instead of the mustard. Any other fish suited for broiling may be substituted for the bass. For 4.

POMPANO IN GARLIC SAUCE

Garlic cloves	3
Olive oil	6 tablespoons
Pompano, whole	2 pounds
Salt and pepper	To taste
Oranges	2
Minced parsley	2 tablespoons

Mash one garlic clove, mix with 3 tablespoons of olive oil and rub on whole clean fish. Sprinkle with salt and pepper and bake in 350° oven for 45 minutes, basting with the juice of one of the oranges.

Fry two other garlic cloves in the rest of the oil, remove garlic cloves and add the juice of the other orange, salt, pepper and minced parsley. Serve hot sauce on fish.

It is better if sour oranges are used, or one tablespoon of lemon juice is added to the sauce. For 2.

MARINATED FISH

Sliced fish	3 pounds
Cooking oil	4 tablespoons
Olive oil	4 tablespoons
Garlic	3 cloves
Onion	1 large
Water	1 cup
Vinegar	1 cup
Toasted coriander seeds	½ teaspoon
Powdered cinnamon	½ teaspoon
Pepper	½ teaspoon
Salt	1 teaspoon
Bay leaves	3
Sliced lemon	1
Olives and long canned Mexican peppers for garnish	

Wash and dry fish slices.

Heat both oils and fry garlic cloves. When dark brown, remove. In same oil fry fish slices until golden brown on both sides; carefully remove and place on brown paper or paper towels. Fry sliced onion until soft, add water, vinegar and spices and cook for a few minutes. Remove from fire and let cool.

Place fish slices on a shallow, large Pyrex dish and cover with sliced onion (the cooked one) vinegar sauce, crumbled bay leaves and sliced lemon. Place in refrigerator for at least two days.

Serve cold with more olive oil and garnish with olives and chiles. For 6 or 8.

Meats

SONORA STEW (*Puchero de Sonora*)

This is a specialty in Sonora, one of the northern states of Mexico, famous for the bravery of its men, its chick-peas and its tomatoes.

Chick-peas	½ pound
Meat for stew	1 pound
Salt	To taste
Large onion	1
String beans	½ pound
Shortening	3 tablespoons
Garlic	1 clove
Tomato sauce	1 cup
Red chili powder	1 tablespoon

Soak chick-peas overnight. Next day boil in plenty of water. When half done, slip off skin and put back in water with the meat (cut in small pieces), salt and onion. When meat is almost tender add string beans (cleaned and tied in bunches).

Melt shortening, add minced garlic, and when transparent add tomato sauce and red chili powder. Cook five minutes and add to the boiling stew. Cook until meat and vegetables are very tender. For 4 or 6.

SHREDDED MEAT (*Ropa Vieja*)

Stew meat	1 pound
Shortening	3 tablespoons
Minced onion	1 teaspoon
Minced garlic	1 clove (optional)
Tomato sauce	1 cup
Chili sauce or powder	1 teaspoon (optional)
Minced parsley	1 teaspoon
Salt and pepper	To taste
Hard-boiled eggs	2
Bread slices	3

Use leftover meat or boil meat, saving stock for making a good soup. After it is boiled, shred it. Melt fat, add onion and garlic and when transparent add tomato sauce, chili sauce and parsley. Cook five minutes, then add shredded meat.

Cook until almost dry. Put on hot platter. Garnish with slices of hard-boiled egg and triangles of bread fried in butter.

Some boiled diced potatoes or other vegetables may be added. For 4 or 6.

DON QUIXOTE SUPPER (*La Cena de Don Quijote*)

Meat for soup or stew	1 pound
Raw ham	¼ pound
Red pimento	1
Minced onion	1 teaspoon
Minced parsley	1 teaspoon
Olive oil	4 tablespoons
Vinegar	2 tablespoons
Salt and pepper	To taste
Paprika	To taste

Boil the meat and ham and save stock for a good soup. When it is tender, cut meat and ham in small pieces. Mix with chopped pimento, onion and parsley. Season well with oil, vinegar, salt and pepper. Place on cold platter and sprinkle with paprika.

Serve very cold and you will have the pleasure of eating what the Spanish Cavalier had for supper "almost every night," according to the famous author Cervantes. For 4 or 6.

MEAT AND POTATO PIE (*Torta de Papa y Carne*)

Meat for soup or stew	1 pound
Fat	2 tablespoons
Minced onion	1 teaspoon
Tomato sauce	1 cup
Minced parsley	1 teaspoon
Minced ham	¼ pound
Salt and pepper	To taste
Mashed potatoes	4 cups
Bread crumbs	3 tablespoons
Butter	2 tablespoons

Boil meat and shred it. Melt fat and add onion; when it is soft, add tomato sauce and parsley. Cook five minutes. Add meat and minced ham. Cook well until almost dry.

Make mashed potatoes according to your favorite recipe.

Butter baking dish, place a layer of mashed potatoes, then the cooked meat and then another layer of the potatoes. Sprinkle with bread crumbs, dot with butter and bake in the oven until brown. For 4 or 6.

MEAT PATTIES (*Tortitas de Carne*)

Minced cooked meat	1 pound
Almonds	12
Raisins	12
Olives	6
Fat	1 tablespoon
Minced onion	1 teaspoon
Tomato sauce (thick)	¼ cup
Minced parsley	1 teaspoon
Dry bread crumbs	4 tablespoons
Milk	2 tablespoons
Egg	1
Salt and pepper	To taste

The meat can be left over from the roast of the day before. Blanch, skin and chop almonds; soak raisins and chop olives.

Melt the fat, fry onion until soft, then add tomato sauce and parsley, bread crumbs, milk, raisins, almonds. Remove from fire and add slightly beaten egg and meat. Form into patties.

FOR FRYING PATTIES

Eggs	3
Flour	1 tablespoon
Hot fat	½ cup

Beat egg whites until stiff. Add yolks, beating all the time. Add sifted flour.

Dip each patty in beaten eggs and fry in hot fat.

Serve accompanied by salad, tomato or avocado sauce. For 4 or 6.

MEAT BALLS (*Albóndigas*)

Ground pork	½ pound
Ground veal	1 pound
Stale bread	¼ cup
Milk	¼ cup
Raw egg	1
Oregano	½ teaspoon
Salt and pepper	To taste
Olives	12 to 15

Pass both meats through food chopper. Mix with bread soaked in milk, raw egg, spices (if any) and salt and pepper.

Form 12 or 15 balls, placing a stoned olive in the center of each. Drop in boiling sauce and cook until done.

SAUCE

Fat	2 tablespoons
Minced onion	1 teaspoon
Minced garlic	1 clove (optional)
Tomato soup	1 can
Chili sauce or powder	1 tablespoon
Parsley	1 tablespoon
Salt	To taste

Melt fat, add minced onion and garlic. When golden brown add tomato soup, chili and a little water and parsley. Cook five minutes. For 4.

MEAT BALLS SAN LUIS POTOSI STYLE
(*Albóndigas Potosinas*)

Ground pork	½ pound
Ground veal	½ pound
Minced onion	1 teaspoon
Minced garlic	1 teaspoon
Boiled rice	½ cup
Powdered cinnamon	1 dash
Cumin seeds	4
Egg	1
Salt and pepper	To taste
Water	1 quart
Carrots	3
Fat	1 tablespoon
Tomato sauce	½ cup
Fresh peach	1
Fresh pear	1
Apple	1
Cornstarch	1 tablespoon
Olive oil	1 tablespoon

Mix ground meat with half of the onion and garlic, boiled rice, cinnamon and cumin seeds and grind again. Mix with raw egg and season mixture with salt and pepper. Form into balls.

Place on fire soup kettle containing water and carrots cut in quarters. Meanwhile melt fat in frying pan and fry remaining onion and garlic until soft, then add tomato sauce. Cook five minutes and add to the soup kettle. When carrots are almost tender add fruits, peeled and cut in pieces, meat balls and cornstarch. When everything is done, add olive oil and serve very hot in a deep platter as there will be plenty of sauce. For 6.

HASH TURNOVERS (*Empanadas de Picadillo*)

Flour	1 pound
Egg	1
Fat	¼ cup
Stock	As needed
Salt	½ teaspoon

Make dough with above ingredients. Work well until soft. Roll thin and cut rounds. Place in center of each round a little hash made with the following recipe; put egg or water on edges and fold. Fry in deep fat until golden brown, or bake in a 350° oven.

HASH

Shortening	¼ cup
Hamburger meat	1 pound
Minced onion	1 tablespoon
Tomato sauce	1 cup
Minced parsley	1 tablespoon
Almonds	18
Raisins	18
Salt	To taste

Heat shortening, add meat and onion; when brown, add tomato sauce and parsley. Cook well and add skinned almonds and raisins (previously soaked in water). Or use chopped olives instead of raisins. For 6 or 8.

MEAT LOAF WITH PRUNES (*Albondigón con Ciruelas*)

Ground veal	2 pounds
Whole egg	1
Egg yolk	1
Salt, pepper and nutmeg	To taste
Flour and butter to fry roll	

SAUCE

Prunes	¼ pound
Red wine	1 cup
Cornstarch	1 teaspoon
Stock	½ cup
Salt and pepper	To taste

Mix ground meat with eggs and season to taste. Form a roll, sprinkle with flour and fry in butter.

Soak prunes, remove pits and mash with the wine. Pour over the meat in the pan. Dilute cornstarch in stock or water and add.

Season with salt and pepper and simmer until meat is done, adding a little more water if necessary. For 8 or 10.

VEAL WITH ONIONS (*Ternera con Cebollas*)

Veal or tender beef, cut in cubes	2 pounds
Large onions, sliced	3
Large tomatoes, chopped	3
Bay leaf	1
Cinnamon	1 stick
Olive oil	1 cup
Vinegar	2 tablespoons
Salt and pepper	To taste

Put all the ingredients in a saucepan and add water to cover. Cook until meat is tender.

Serve very hot without straining sauce. For 6 or 8.

SPANISH MENESTRA (*Menestra a la Española*)

Olive oil	½ cup
Ham	¼ pound
Spanish or pork sausages	2
Garlic	2 cloves
Tomatoes	1 small can
Saffron	1 pinch
Cinnamon	1 dash
Salt and pepper	To taste
Veal cut in cubes	2 pounds
Lima beans	½ pound
Artichokes	3
Fish	3 slices
Hard-boiled eggs	3

Heat oil in pan; add cubed ham and sliced sausage. Remove and keep warm. In the same oil fry garlic cloves and chopped tomatoes, adding saffron, cinnamon, salt and pepper. Add cubed veal and some water. Cook until meat is half done, then add sausages, ham, boiled lima beans, boiled artichokes cut in half and pieces of fish, cleaned and fried in a little oil. Season well with salt and pepper and cook until thick. Garnish with slices of hard-boiled egg. For 6 or 8.

VEAL STEW GUADALAJARA (SPAIN)
(*Guiso de Ternera Estilo Guadalajara*)

Onions	2
Veal stew meat	2 pounds
Garlic cloves	2
Bay leaf	1
Thyme	1 sprig
Olive oil	2 tablespoons
White wine	1 cup
Parsley	1 sprig
Salt and pepper	To taste

Slice onions and put with meat and other ingredients in a well covered pan. Cook until tender. Remove garlic before serving. For 6 or 8.

VEAL WITH WALNUT SAUCE
(*Ternera con Salsa de Nueces*)

Slices of veal	3 pounds
Flour	½ cup
Salt and pepper	To taste
Fat	½ cup
Stock or hot water	3 cups
Minced onion	1 tablespoon
Bread soaked in vinegar	1 slice
Walnuts	20
Garlic	1 clove
Sherry wine	½ cup

Pound the meat well with a rolling pin. Roll in flour, salt and pepper and fry until brown. Turn into another pan; add water or stock and cook gently.

In the remaining fat, fry onion, and when soft add bread soaked in vinegar, ground nuts, garlic and sherry wine. Mix to a paste.

Add to the meat and cook until meat is very tender. Serve very hot. For 6 or 8.

VEAL ROLL (*Rollo de Ternera*)

Thin slices of veal leg	2 pounds
Ground beef	½ pound
Ground ham	¼ pound
Dry bread crumbs	½ cup
Hard-boiled eggs	2
Sausage meat	¼ pound
Flour	¼ cup
Salt and pepper	To taste
Fat	3 tablespoons
Carrots	12
Stock or water	1 cup
Sherry wine	½ cup

Place veal slices on a board. Spread on them a mixture of the ground beef, minced ham, bread crumbs, hard-boiled eggs, sausage meat, salt and pepper. Roll and skewer. Roll in flour and fry until brown. Turn into another pan and in the same fat fry carrots (sliced), adding them to the meat with the remaining fat. Add stock or water and sherry wine. Cook gently until meat is done. Serve meat rolls on platter with carrots; serve the sauce separately in a sauce-boat. For 6 or 8.

VEAL VALENCIA STYLE (*Ternera a la Valenciana*)

Leg of veal	2 pounds
Ham	¼ pound
Bacon	¼ pound
Tomatoes	3
Rice	½ cup
Salt and pepper	To taste
Peas	1 cup
Red canned pimentos	2

Cut veal in cubes, as well as ham and bacon. Fry in a little fat and when brown add chopped tomatoes. Cook ten minutes, then add 2 cups of water and washed rice, salt and pepper. When rice is almost done, add peas. Serve hot, garnished with pimento strips. For 4 or 6.

VEAL DE LUXE (*Ternera de Lujo*)

Veal	2 pounds
Pork	¼ pound
Sausage	¼ pound
Chicken breast	1
Fat	3 tablespoons
Carrots	3
Onion	1
Bay leaf	1
Whole black peppercorns	2
Water	1 quart
Cloves	2
Salt and pepper	To taste
Cream	1 cup
Cooked beets	3
Hard-boiled egg	1

Fry veal and pork in fat until brown. Add the rest of the ingredients except cream, beets and egg. Cook gently until meat is tender. Reserve the meat.

Strain the sauce. Take sausage meat, breast of chicken and pork meat and pass through food chopper, moistening with the cream. Cook mixture and if too thick add a little milk.

Place strained sauce in hot platter, then sliced hot veal. Cover with ground-meat mixture and garnish with sliced beets and chopped egg. For 6 or 8.

MUTTON WITH TURNIPS (*Carnero con Nabos*)

Mutton cut in pieces	2 pounds
Fat	3 tablespoons
Turnips (white)	12
Flour	1 tablespoon
Onion	1
Parsley	1 sprig
Bay leaf	1
Cloves	2
Hot water	2 cups
White wine	1 cup
Salt and pepper	To taste

Melt fat. Brown meat and turn into another pan. In the same fat fry turnips cut in quarters, drain and add to the meat. In the remaining fat brown the flour, dilute with the water and add to the meat with the onion, parsley, bay leaf, cloves, salt and pepper.

Cook until meat is tender. Ten minutes before serving add the wine. For 4 or 6.

LEG OF LAMB WITH CABBAGE
(*Pierna de Cordero con Col*)

Leg of lamb	1
Fat	3 tablespoons
Salt and pepper	To taste
Hot water	1 cup
Tomatoes	1 small can
White wine	1 cup
Onion	1
Garlic	2 cloves
White cabbage	1
Anise seeds	½ teaspoon
Butter	½ cup

Clean leg and rub with fat, salt and pepper. Place in baking pan in 350° oven. When brown add hot water, tomatoes, wine, onion and garlic. Bake until done.

Boil cabbage with anise seeds. Slice very fine and add to the meat with the butter ten minutes before serving. For 6 or 8.

LAMB CHOPS MASQUERADE
(*Costillas de Cordero Carnaval*)

Potatoes	2 pounds
Milk	2 tablespoons
Egg yolks	2
Salt and pepper	To taste
Tender lamb chops	8
Dry bread crumbs	1 cup
Eggs	2
Shortening	½ cup

Boil potatoes, pass through ricer; add milk and egg yolks
and season well with salt and pepper. Boil the chops with
very little water, wipe with a clean cloth and cover each
chop well with the mashed potatoes, pressing with the
hands so that the potatoes stick well to the meat. Leave the
end of the bone sticking out. Roll in dry crumbs, then in
beaten eggs and again in dry crumbs. Fry in the hot fat
until brown on both sides. Serve immediately with a green
vegetable or salad. Trim bones with paper frills. For 4 to 8.

LEG OF LAMB WITH RED WINE
(*Pierna de Cordero con Vino*)

Leg of lamb	1	
Ham	¼	pound
Raw carrots	2	
Garlic	2	cloves (optional)
Fat	½	cup
Cinnamon	⅛	teaspoon
Peppercorns	3	
Cloves	2	
Vinegar	½	cup
Hot water	½	cup
Red wine	1	cup
Caramelized sugar	1	teaspoon
Salt and pepper	To taste	

Lard the leg of lamb with strips of the ham, strips of carrot
and pieces of garlic. Melt fat and brown the meat. Mash
spices in a mortar and mix with the vinegar. Pour over
meat with hot water, wine and caramelized sugar. Cover
and cook over slow fire or in 350° oven until done. For
6 or 8.

CASSEROLE OF BREADED CUTLETS
(*Cacerola de Costillas Empanizadas*)

Breaded veal or pork cutlets	8
Fat	2 tablespoons
Onion	1 teaspoon
Chopped tomatoes	2 cups
Minced parsley	1 teaspoon
Romaine lettuce	1 leaf (optional)
Salt and pepper	To taste

Prepare breaded cutlets as usual and fry in fat. Melt the 2 tablespoons of fat and fry onion; when soft add tomatoes and parsley. Cook five minutes and add lettuce, sliced very fine. Cook 5 minutes more, seasoning well with salt and pepper. Put some of this in the casserole dish, then two of the breaded cutlets, another layer of sauce and again a layer of meat. The last layer should be of sauce. Bake in hot oven 20 to 30 minutes. Serve very hot. For 8.

PORK CHOPS WITH AVOCADO SAUCE
(*Costillas de Puerco con Guacamole*)

Pork chops	8
Salt	To taste
Vinegar	2 tablespoons
Dry bread crumbs	1 cup
Eggs	2
Fat	½ cup

Sprinkle the chops with salt and vinegar; dip in bread crumbs, then in beaten eggs and again in bread crumbs, pressing well with hands. Fry in hot fat over slow fire until well browned on each side. Serve hot with Avocado Sauce. (See RICE section.) For 8.

STUFFED PORK (*Puerco Relleno*)

Pork loin	2 pounds
Fat	¼ cup
Minced onion	1 teaspoon
Tomato	1
Cooked spinach	1 cup
Minced ham	1 cup
Salt and pepper	To taste
Hard-boiled egg	1

Clean meat and open a slit in center to form a bag. Heat half of the fat and fry onion until soft; add chopped tomato, chopped spinach and ham. Season with salt and pepper, remove from fire and add chopped hard-boiled egg.

Stuff meat with this mixture and skewer. Fry in the remaining fat until well browned. Place in baking pan with one cup of hot water. Bake until tender and serve with tomato sauce. For 4 to 6.

PORK CHOPS WITH WINE SAUCE
(*Costillas de Puerco con Vino*)

Garlic cloves	2
Bread	1 slice
Parsley	1 bunch
Stock	1 cup
Red wine	1 cup
Salt and pepper	To taste
Pork chops	8

Mash the cloves, bread and parsley to paste. Add stock and wine and season well. Melt a little fat and cook this sauce several minutes. Then strain and serve with the fried chops. For 8.

GLAZED PORK (*Lomo de Puerco Acaramelado*)

Pork loin	2 pounds
Olive oil	½ cup
White wine	1 cup
Sugar	3 tablespoons
Salt	To taste

Fry meat in the oil until brown, adding salt to taste. Then add wine, sugar and salt and cook slowly until brown and glazed. For 4.

MOCHOMOS (*Special Dish from Chihuahua, Mexico*)

Pork meat	2 pounds
Fat	2 tablespoons
Avocado sauce	2 cups

Boil the meat in a little water so that when it is done there is no water left. Shred meat very fine and fry in melted fat until dry and crisp. Do this shortly before serving. Serve in the center of round platter and put Avocado Sauce (page 36) around it. For 4 or 6.

MEAT ROLLS WITH PEANUT BUTTER

Small minute steaks or thin slices of tender meat	12
Salt and pepper	To taste
Boiled ham	3 slices (thin)
Shortening	3 tablespoons
Minced onion	2 tablespoons
Thick tomato purée	4 tablespoons
Peanut butter	4 tablespoons
Water	½ cup

Pound meat until very thin, sprinkle with salt and pepper and place a piece of ham on each slice. Roll and secure with string or toothpick.

Fry in hot shortening until light golden brown, add minced onion and tomato purée, then peanut butter diluted in water. Cover and cook until meat is very tender. Serve with steamed or baked potatoes. For 6.

BRAZILIAN BEEF FILLETS   (*Filetes a la Brasileña*)

Tenderloin steaks	6
Vinegar	1 tablespoon
Salt and pepper	To taste
Fat	2 tablespoons
Minced onion	1 tablespoon
Minced garlic	1 clove
Tomatoes	1 No. 2 can
Minced parsley	1 tablespoon

TO FRY FILLETS

Eggs	3
Salt	½ teaspoon
Flour	2 tablespoons
Fat	½ cup

A few hours before serving place fillets in the refrigerator with vinegar, salt and pepper.

Thirty minutes before serving, melt the fat (2 tablespoons) and fry fillets in a large frying pan, about three minutes on each side. Remove from pan and put in casserole; cover and keep warm.

In the fat left in the pan fry the onion and garlic; when transparent, add chopped tomatoes and parsley. Cook five minutes and add to the casserole. Cover.

Beat egg whites until stiff, add the yolks, one by one, beating after each addition, and add salt. Drain fillets from sauce, sprinkle with flour, dip in egg and fry in hot fat until brown.

Serve hot on platter and put hot sauce in sauceboat. For 6.

VEAL WITH TUNA FISH SAUCE
(*Ternera con Salsa de Atún*)

Veal	2 pounds
Tuna fish	1 can
Anchovy fillets	2
Hard-boiled egg yolks	3
Mustard	1 teaspoon
Olive oil	2 tablespoons
Lemon juice	2 teaspoons
Peppercorns	2
Cloves	2
Minced parsley	1 teaspoon
Capers	3 tablespoons
Salt and pepper	To taste
Watercress	1 bunch

Boil the meat with a bouquet of herbs; sage is especially good. Add peppercorns and cloves to taste. When very tender, slice, and place on platter.

Mash tuna fish and anchovy fillets with a fork and mix with egg yolks, mustard, olive oil and lemon juice until very smooth. Season well and add minced parsley and capers. Cover meat with tuna mixture and garnish with watercress. Serve very cold. For 4 or 6.

MEAT BALLS WITH CHEESE

Ground pork	1 pound
Ground veal or beef	1 pound
Hot sausage	1 piece (about 3 inches)
Grated cheese	1 cup
Hard-boiled eggs	2
Raw eggs	2
Fresh or canned tomatoes	2
Minced onion	1 tablespoon
Shortening	2 tablespoons
Minced parsley	1 tablespoon
Saffron, cloves, pepper	1 pinch each
Salt	To taste

Mix meats with sausage (without skin), grated cheese, chopped hard-boiled eggs, beaten raw eggs, chopped tomatoes, onion (fried in the shortening), minced parsley, herbs and salt to taste. Mix well and make balls the size of a walnut and roll well in flour. Drop in the boiling sauce until well cooked.

SAUCE

Shortening	2 tablespoons
Stale bread	1 slice
Green pepper	1
Minced onion	1 tablespoon
Tomato purée	3 tablespoons
Stock or water	3 cups
Salt	To taste

Melt shortening, fry bread slice. In same shortening, fry chopped green pepper and onion; when soft add tomato purée. When well fried add stock or water, fried mashed bread, and salt. For 6 or 8.

CHILE CON CARNE

Red kidney beans	1 pound
Whole onion	1
Salt	To taste
Stew meat	2 pounds
Bay leaf	1 piece
Shortening	3 tablespoons
Minced onion	2 tablespoons
Fresh or canned tomatoes	4 cups
Chili powder	1 tablespoon
or canned mole powder	2 tablespoons
Marjoram or oregano	1 pinch
Cornstarch	1 teaspoon

Soak beans overnight. Next morning boil with plenty of water, whole onion and a little salt. When half done add meat cut in pieces and continue cooking until both beans and meat are very soft (it can be done in pressure cooker). Add salt and bay leaf, and cook a little more.

Heat shortening, fry minced onion; when soft add chopped tomatoes and chili powder. (If mole powder is used, it has to be fried before tomatoes.) When this is well fried, add beans and meat, adding marjoram or oregano, and cornstarch diluted in a little cold water. Cook until thick and of creamlike consistency.

Serve hot with tortillas. For 6 or 8.

HAMBURGER MEAT WITH CHILE AND BEANS

Red kidney beans	1 pound
Whole onion	1
Salt	To taste
Shortening	4 tablespoons
Minced onion	2 tablespoons
Chili powder	1 tablespoon
or canned mole powder	3 tablespoons
Hamburger meat	2 pounds
Fresh or canned tomatoes	4
Cornstarch	2 tablespoons
Bay leaf	1 piece
Marjoram or dried oregano	1 pinch

Soak beans overnight. Next morning boil in plenty of water with whole onion, salt and 1 tablespoon shortening, until beans are very soft. (This can be done in pressure cooker.)

Heat the other three tablespoons of shortening, fry minced onion; when soft add chili or mole powder and meat, cooking until pink of meat disappears. Add chopped tomatoes and when well fried put in cornstarch diluted in a little cold water, herbs, salt to taste and beans with part of their liquor. Let cook until it thickens. Serve with hot tortillas. For 6 or 8.

FILLET OF BEEF WITH CARROTS

Butter	¼ pound
Young carrots	18
Large onion	1
Fillet of beef	6 thick slices
Flour	2 tablespoons
Salt and pepper	To taste
Stock	½ cup
Minced parsley	3 tablespoons

Melt butter and fry sliced carrots. Add sliced or chopped onion. When both are transparent, add beef fillets sprinkled with flour, salt and pepper. When flour turns golden brown, add stock (that can be made with water and bouillon cube). Place over another pan containing hot water and steam until meat is very tender. Serve at once, sprinkled with parsley. For 6.

BEEF FILLET WITH RED WINE

Fillet of beef in one piece	2 pounds
Bacon	1 thick slice
Garlic	1 clove
Parsley (chopped)	¼ cup
Salt and pepper	To taste
Shortening	3 tablespoons
Red wine	1 cup
Water	1 cup

Lard fillet of beef with thin strips of bacon. Mash garlic with parsley, salt and pepper, or put in liquidizer or blender with a little water.

Rub fillet with this paste and place in roaster with

shortening. When brown on all sides, baste with wine and water. Keep in the oven until desired doneness is obtained.

Serve very hot with sauce in a gravy boat and accompanied by steamed potatoes with melted butter and minced parsley. For 6.

ROLL OF FILLET OF BEEF

Opened fillet of beef	2 pounds
Salt and pepper	To taste
Vinegar	1 tablespoon
Eggs	3
Red pimentos	2
Shortening	3 tablespoons
Minced onion	1 tablespoon
Piñon nuts (shelled)	4 tablespoons
Garlic	½ a small clove
Parsley	1 tablespoon
Flour	2 tablespoons
Stock or water	2 cups

Ask the butcher to open the meat like a sheet. Season with salt and pepper and sprinkle vinegar on the surface.

Beat eggs and make a large thin omelet. Cut it in strips and place in rows over the extended meat, alternating with pimentos, also cut in strips. Roll like a jelly roll and tie with a string.

Melt shortening and fry meat until golden brown on all sides. Remove meat and in remaining shortening, fry chopped onion and a paste made from mashing the shelled piñon nuts, garlic clove, chopped parsley, and flour. After a few seconds add meat stock or water, salt and pepper.

Place meat in baking pan or roaster with sauce. Cover and bake in hot oven (400° F.) until meat is tender.

Serve sliced and covered with hot sauce.

Piñones are tiny nuts in the shape of pecans but very small. They grow in the cone of a certain pine tree and are sometimes called pignolia and sold in packages. If piñones are not obtainable, use blanched almonds or pecans instead. For 6.

FILLET OF BEEF WITH GRAPES

Whole fillet of beef	2 pounds
Salt and pepper	To taste
Shortening	4 tablespoons
Fresh or canned tomatoes	3
Onion	1
Water	1 cup
Dry sherry	4 tablespoons
Worcestershire sauce	2 tablespoons
Prepared mustard	1 teaspoon
Cornstarch	1 tablespoon
Seedless grapes (green variety)	1½ pounds

After cleaning fillet of beef, sprinkle with salt and pepper and cover with shortening, if it is liquid like oil, or rub the surface with it, if it is lard or vegetable shortening. Put chopped tomatoes and sliced onion on top and place in hot oven (400° F.), basting from time to time with a mixture of water, sherry wine, Worcestershire sauce and mustard.

Bake for about an hour, or less if wanted rare (taking into consideration that it has to go into the oven again with the grapes for about 15 minutes).

Strain the juice from baking pan into another small pan and add cornstarch diluted in a little cold water. Add more salt if necessary. Cook for a few minutes.

Place bunches of washed grapes on the fillet, securing them with toothpicks. Cover with sauce (pouring it over the grapes) and return to the oven for 15 minutes or until grapes are plump and well heated. Transfer to a hot platter and carve at the table, serving a small bunch of grapes to each person. Or carve in the kitchen and place the bunch of grapes on top. Besides being delicious, this is a very spectacular dish. For 6.

BROILED MEAT TAMPICO STYLE

Opened fillet of beef	2 pounds
Shortening	3 tablespoons
Sliced onion	1 cup
Strips of Poblano pepper or	
green pepper	1 cup
Salt and pepper	To taste
Small enchiladas	12
Fried crispy beans	2 cups
Avocado sauce	2 cups

Ask the butcher to open the meat like a sheet and to pound it until very thin.

Melt shortening and fry slices of onion and strips of Poblano pepper or of green pepper until both are very soft. Season with salt.

Prepare Tomato Enchiladas as in recipe in the chapter on Tortillas.

Prepare mashed fried crispy beans as in recipe in the chapter on Vegetables.

Prepare avocado sauce as in recipe for White Rice with Avocado Sauce.

Have grill or heavy skillet very hot and a few minutes before serving cut meat in six pieces, sprinkle with salt and pepper. Put a little shortening on the grill and cook meat a few minutes on each side.

Serve on each plate a piece of meat, two enchiladas, some green peppers with onion, and a little avocado sauce. For 6.

Minute steaks can be used instead of the fillet of beef.

BRAISED LAMB

Leg of lamb cut in large pieces	2 pounds
Raw ham	1 slice
Garlic	1 clove
Blanched almonds	3 tablespoons
Seeded raisins	2 tablespoons
Shortening	3 tablespoons
Fresh or canned tomatoes	4
Sherry wine	1 cup
Salt and pepper	To taste
Cloves and cinnamon	⅛ teaspoon each
Chili powder	⅛ teaspoon

Lard meat with ham strips, slivers of garlic, slivers of blanched almonds, and whole raisins.

Fry pieces of meat in hot shortening and cover with chopped tomatoes, wine, salt and spices. Cover well and cook over a very slow fire until meat is very tender.

Serve accompanied with white rice. For 4 or 6.

LOIN OF PORK WITH SPINACH

Loin of pork	2 pounds
Lemon, salt and pepper	To taste
Chili powder	To taste (optional)
Shortening	4 tablespoons
Chopped onion	1 tablespoon
Garlic	1 small clove (optional)
Cooked chopped spinach	2 cups
Cooked chopped ham	¼ pound
Hard-boiled eggs	3
Raw egg	1
Sliced onion	1
Water	2 cups
Bay leaf	1 piece
Marjoram and thyme	1 pinch each

Open meat in one big piece, sprinkle with salt and pepper or chili powder and lemon juice.

Heat two tablespoons of shortening and fry chopped onion, garlic and cooked chopped spinach. Remove from fire and mix chopped ham, chopped hard-boiled eggs and raw egg. Season to taste. Spread this on meat, roll and secure with string. Fry until golden brown. Place on a roasting pan, cover with sliced onion and water and bake until well cooked. About 20 minutes before taking out of the oven, sprinkle with herbs. Baste and turn frequently.

For serving, remove string and slice. Serve hot sauce in the sauceboat. For 4 to 6.

LOIN OF PORK WITH PRUNES

Loin of pork	2 pounds
Cooked prunes	10
Salt and pepper	To taste
Garlic	2 cloves
Sliced onion	1
Shortening	3 tablespoons
Tomato purée	1 cup
Water	1 cup
Bay leaf	1
Marjoram	1 pinch
Red wine	1 cup

Clean and wipe meat. Make an incision all along the center of the loin and insert pitted prunes. Sprinkle with salt and pepper and fry with whole garlic cloves and sliced onion. When golden brown add tomato purée and cook a few minutes longer. Remove garlic cloves, add water, cover and cook on slow fire until meat is tender. Add bay leaf, marjoram and wine and cook a little longer.

If sauce should dry before the meat is well cooked, add more water. On the other hand, if meat is tender and sauce is too thin, add a teaspoon of cornstarch, diluted in a little cold water, letting the sauce boil for a while.

It can be served with small potatoes, boiled, fried and sprinkled with chopped parsley. For 4 to 6.

LOIN OF PORK WITH PINEAPPLE JUICE

Loin of pork	2 pounds
Salt and pepper	To taste
Powdered dry oregano	¼ teaspoon
Ground ham	2 cups
Shortening	3 tablespoons
Pineapple juice	2 cups

Open loin of pork to make a thin sheet. Sprinkle with salt, pepper and oregano. Spread with ground ham, roll and tie with string.

Brown on all sides, pour on pineapple juice and cook, covered, over slow fire until meat is tender. Add more juice or water if necessary and add more salt if needed.

It can be served with sweet potatoes and romaine salad. For 4 to 6.

LOIN OF PORK WITH MILK

Loin of pork	2 pounds
Salt and pepper	To taste
Shortening	3 tablespoons
Milk	2 cups
Dry bread crumbs	1 cup
Minced parsley	2 tablespoons

Clean and wipe meat. Sprinkle with salt and pepper and brown in hot shortening.

Place on baking pan and cover with half a cup of scalded milk. When reduced, add another half cup and so on until the two cups are used.

The last cup should be mixed with the crumbs, salt and pepper, and poured over the meat. Keep in the oven until golden brown.

Serve hot, sprinkled with minced parsley and with a nice salad. For 4.

SHREDDED PORK MEAT (*Tinga*)

Loin of pork	1½ pounds
Potatoes	1 pound
Shortening	3 tablespoons
Large onion	1
Hot sausage	½ pound
Chopped tomatoes	3
Salt	To taste
Chipotle (small dry, red chile, pickled)	1 (optional)
Avocado	1

Boil meat with salt in enough water to cover, until tender.

Boil potatoes with jackets in salted water until well cooked but not mushy. Peel and dice.

Heat shortening and fry half of the onion (chopped). Before it turns brown, add crumbled sausage (skin removed). When it begins to get crispy, add chopped tomatoes, and cook for a few minutes. Add diced potatoes and shredded meat. Season with salt and a little dried oregano if desired. Lastly add chipotle cut in small pieces or, if not available, a little chili powder.

Meanwhile slice other half of onion and put in salted water. When Tinga is almost dry, serve, garnished with onion rings and sliced avocado. It should be taken with hot tortillas.

This is a good stuffing for tacos. For 6 or 8.

COLD MEAT PLATTER (*Fiambre*)

Fresh or smoked tongue	1 (small)
Pig's feet	4
Loin of pork	1 pound
Chicken	1
Olive oil	½ cup
Vinegar	¼ cup
Salt and pepper	To taste
Lettuce or romaine	1 head
Fresh tomatoes	4
Large onion	1
Olives and radish roses	To garnish
Avocados	2
Dried oregano	To taste
Long, light chiles in vinegar (canned)	To taste
Small fried tortillas	

The day before serving, boil tongue until very tender. Boil pig's feet until meat falls apart from bones. This takes several hours unless these meats are cooked in pressure cooker. Loin of pork can also be cooked the day before, until very tender.

Place chicken in a saucepan with carrots, onion, celery leaf, etc., to make a nice consommé. Let cool overnight and next morning take off fat that has come up to the surface. For serving consommé, a little Accent and meat extract can be added for flavor and color.

Marinate all the meats overnight in oil, vinegar, salt and pepper.

The day after, shortly before serving, clean romaine and shred, skin and slice tomatoes (removing seeds), slice onion and put in salted water.

On a large platter, place shredded romaine with a little oil and vinegar. On top of romaine, place: pieces of boned chicken, pieces of pig's feet, sliced loin of pork and sliced and skinned tongue. The meats can be mixed or placed with tomato slices separating the different kinds.

Garnish with olives, radish roses and avocado slices.

In small dishes serve: powdered oregano, chopped onion and chiles or chili powder.

In Mexico this dish is eaten with fried small tortillas instead of bread.

It is a very nice dish for a party. With the consommé, dessert and coffee it is a complete dinner. For 8 or 10.

LAMB TONGUES WITH OLIVES
(*Lengüetas de Cordero con Aceitunas*)

Lamb tongues	6
Fat	¼ cup
Minced onion	1 tablespoon
Tomatoes	3
Minced parsley	1 tablespoon
Water	1 cup
Salt and pepper	To taste
Cornstarch	1 tablespoon
Stuffed olives	12
Capers	2 tablespoons
Small tortillas	12

Boil tongues until tender enough to skin. Cool, skin, and roll, sewing with needle and thread. Fry rolls in half of the fat, add onion and when transparent add chopped tomatoes, parsley, water, salt and pepper. When tongues are very tender remove and strain sauce, adding cornstarch with a little water, olives and capers. Cook five minutes and add, very hot, to the tongue rolls in platter.

In the rest of the fat fry small tortillas until crisp and serve with tongues. For 6.

TONGUE WITH ORANGE SAUCE
(Lengua en Salsa de Naranja)

Beef tongue	1
Bay leaf	1
Peppercorns	3
Sherry	⅓ cup
Vinegar	2 tablespoons
Salt	To taste
Oranges	4
Butter	2 tablespoons
Ham (diced)	¼ pound

Boil tongue until tender enough to skin. Put back in pan and add bay leaf, peppercorns, wine, vinegar and salt. When very tender, slice and add the juice of two oranges and the butter. Cook until sauce is thick; strain. Add diced ham. Serve on hot platter. Pour sauce over and garnish with sliced oranges. For 4 or 6.

STUFFED COLD TONGUE (*Lengua Rellena*)

Beef tongue	1
Ground pork	½ pound
Sausage meat	½ pound
Minced ham	½ pound
Hard-boiled eggs	2
Raw eggs	2
Minced parsley	1 teaspoon
Salt and pepper	To taste
Herbs	To taste
Vinegar	1 teaspoon

Clean well a raw tongue and open a pocket almost through

the length of it. Mix all the ingredients (except herbs and vinegar) and stuff tongue; sew opening with thread. Boil in water with vinegar and herbs until tender. Skin and press into a brick-shaped mold. When cold slice and serve with tartare sauce. For 6 or 8.

TRIPE ANDALUCIA (*Callos a la Andaluza*)

Spanish chick-peas	½ pound
Clean tripe	1 pound
Pig's feet	2
Fat	3 tablespoons
Minced onion	1 tablespoon
Minced garlic	1 clove
Minced parsley	1 tablespoon
Tomato sauce	2 cups
Water	2 cups
Salt and pepper	To taste
Bay leaf	1
Thyme and marjoram	1 sprig each
Red pimento	2
Potatoes	3

Soak chick-peas overnight. Next morning boil. Clean tripe and pig's feet and boil until tender.

Melt fat, fry onion, garlic and parsley, add tomato sauce and cook five minutes; add water, salt, pepper and herbs. In this sauce put diced tripe and pig's feet without bones and cut in small pieces. Add boiled and skinned chick-peas, and peeled diced potatoes. Cook everything together for one hour, adding water or stock if necessary. Garnish with pimento strips and serve very hot. For 4 or 6.

Poultry

ORIGIN OF MOLE

ACCORDING to tradition, this dish, which has become the national dish of Mexico, was created by the Mother Superior of a convent of the city of Puebla (the home of the Chile Poblano).

The nuns of the convent were expecting the visit of their bishop and they wanted to treat him with something very special.

The Mother Superior was a good cook, and she thought of making a turkey stew, but in order to improve it, she started frying chiles . . . and then a few almonds . . . and then a few raisins and a little cinnamon and a piece of chocolate. She told one of the nuns to grind the whole thing on the *metate*.

She went to supervise other things and when she came back, the poor nun was still grinding, so the Mother Superior said: "You poor soul, grinding and grinding." The verb to grind in

Spanish is *moler*, so *mole* became the name of the improvised dish, which made the delight of the bishop, and of many generations to come.

Of course, there are as many different kinds of moles almost as there are different families or cooks in Mexico. As with the curries in India, each family has its own favorite.

TURKEY MOLE (*Mole de Guajolote o Pavo*)

6- to 8-pound turkey	1
Toasted almonds	12
Toasted sesame seeds	1 tablespoon
Stale bread, toasted	1 slice
Raisins	12
Ground semi-sweet chocolate	1 tablespoon (optional)
Ground cloves	⅛ teaspoon
Powdered cinnamon	1 teaspoon
Anise seed	¼ teaspoon
Red chili powder	3 to 6 tablespoons
Fat	6 tablespoons
Minced onion	1
Garlic	1 clove
Flour	2 tablespoons
Tomato sauce	3 cups
Salt	To taste

Cut turkey as for fricassee and boil until tender.

Pass through fine food chopper toasted almonds, sesame seeds, toasted bread, raisins and chocolate; mix well with the ground spices and chili powder.

Melt fat, add onion and garlic. When transparent, add flour and when brown, add ground ingredients. Cook until well mixed and smooth and then add tomato sauce. Cook five minutes, add three or four cups of stock (in which turkey was boiled) and salt. Cook a few minutes and then add turkey pieces. Cook gently until thick. Serve with a sprinkling of toasted sesame seeds.

This dish is made in Mexico with dried red chiles soaked and ground, but this recipe is a good substitute.

In large cities it is possible to get mole sauce prepared in cans. All one has to do, then, is to dilute the paste with some turkey stock and add to the meat. For 6 or 8.

Substitute chicken for turkey if desired.

SPICED COLD TURKEY (*Cunete de Pavo*)

6- to 8-pound turkey	1
Fat	3 tablespoons
Carrots	8
Spanish onions	3
White turnips	5
Olive oil	4 cups
Vinegar	5 cups
Peppercorns	6
Cloves	3
Bay leaf	1
Thyme	1 sprig
Marjoram	1 sprig
Salt	To taste

Cut turkey in pieces and fry in hot fat with carrots, onions and turnips (cut in 4). Place in deep enameled pan with oil, vinegar, herbs and spices. Cover tightly and cook gently for several hours, shaking the pan from time to time to avoid scorching. When tender, cool in the same pan. Place in refrigerator. Serve cold, garnished with pimento strips, sliced avocados, olives, radish roses, or pickles.

It is excellent for a cold supper or picnic, and will keep for several days in the refrigerator. For 4.

CHICKEN WITH GREEN PEPPERS
(*Pollo con Chiles Poblanos*)

3- to 4-pound chicken	1
Green peppers	4
Fat	3 tablespoons
Minced onion	2 tablespoons
Minced garlic	1 clove (optional)
Tomato soup	1 cup
Minced parsley	1 tablespoon
Soda	¼ teaspoon
Milk	1 quart
Cornstarch	2 tablespoons
Salt and pepper	To taste

Cut chicken as for fricassee and boil until tender.

Boil green peppers 15 minutes and cut in strips. Heat fat, add onion and garlic; when transparent, add tomato soup, parsley and soda. Cook 5 minutes and add green peppers and milk with cornstarch (diluted). After a few minutes add chicken with a little of the stock. Season well. Sauce should be of a creamy consistency. For 4.

CHICKENS IN RED WINE (*Pollitos en Vino Rojo*)

2½-pound chickens	2
Olive oil	½ cup
Vinegar	½ cup
Onion	1
Garlic	2 cloves
Herbs	1 bouquet
Salt and pepper	To taste
Bacon	¼ pound
Tomatoes	1 No. 2 can
Spring onions	1 bunch
Carrots	2
Red wine	½ bottle

Cut chickens in pieces and marinate for 24 hours in the oil, vinegar, sliced onion, whole garlic, herbs, salt and pepper.

Cut bacon in cubes, place on fire and in the fat cook the chopped tomatoes, spring onions and chopped carrots. Cook five minutes, add the chicken and the strained marinade, then the wine. Cook gently until chickens are tender. For 4 or 6.

CHICKEN CASSEROLE (*Cacerola de Pollo*)

3- to 4-pound chicken (cut in pieces)	1
Cornmeal	½ cup
Fat	½ cup
Spring onions	1 bunch
Small carrots	6
Stock	1 cup
White wine	1 cup
Salt and pepper	To taste

Make the stock with the chicken wings, liver, etc. Cover each piece of chicken thoroughly with cornmeal and fry in hot fat. Place in casserole.

In the remaining fat fry whole onions and quartered carrots; add to the casserole together with stock, wine, salt and pepper. Cook gently until chicken is tender. For 2 or 4.

FRIED CHICKEN SONORA STYLE
(*Pollo Frito Estilo Sonora*)

Potatoes	1 pound
Small green squashes (calabacitas)	½ pound
Tomatoes	1 No. 2 can
Minced onion	1 teaspoon
Olive oil	3 tablespoons
Vinegar	1 tablespoon
Salt and pepper	To taste
Young chicken	1
Romaine	1 head
Oregano	To taste
Chili powder	To taste

Boil, peel, slice and fry the potatoes in hot fat. Boil and slice the squash. Chop the tomatoes and mix with the minced onion, olive oil and vinegar.

If the chicken is very tender, fry directly in deep fat; if not tender, boil first and then fry until brown. (Keep warm.)

For serving, place chicken on a hot platter, place hot potatoes and sliced squash on top, then the cold tomato sauce and finally the shredded romaine and a sprinkling of oregano and chili powder. For 4.

HOT CHICKEN WITH FRUITS (*Mancha Manteles*)

Young chicken (3 to 4 pounds)	1
Pork loin	½ pound
Fat	¼ cup
Almonds	12
Sesame seeds	1 tablespoon
Tomato sauce	2 cups
Red chili powder	1 tablespoon
Cinnamon	⅛ teaspoon
Sugar	1 tablespoon
Pineapple	2 slices
Apples	2
Bananas	2
Boiled sweet potatoes	½ pound
Salt	To taste

Cut chicken in pieces and meat in cubes. Brown in hot fat, drain and change to another pan. In the same fat fry the blanched almonds and the sesame seeds; when brown, mash and return to the frying pan, adding tomato sauce and chili powder, cinnamon and sugar. Cook 5 minutes, add salt and water. Strain sauce and turn into pan with chicken and meat. Cook until tender.

When almost done add pineapple cut in wedges, peeled, cored and sliced apples, sliced but *not peeled* bananas, and boiled, sliced and peeled sweet potatoes. For 4.

SWEET CHICKEN WITH FRUITS (*Tapado de Pollo*)

Young chicken (3 to 4 pounds)	1
Fat	2 tablespoons
Tomatoes	3
Large onions	2
Apples	2
Bananas	2
Peas	1 cup
Green small squash	½ pound
Pineapple	2 slices
Salt, pepper and sugar	To taste
Olive oil	¼ cup

Cut chicken in small pieces. Fry in fat until brown. Oil a casserole and arrange alternate layers of chicken, sliced tomatoes, sliced onions, sliced apples, sliced bananas (with peel), peas, squash, pineapple, salt, pepper, a little bit of sugar and some oil. Cover and bake or cook gently until chicken is very tender.

Pork loin slices may be used instead of chicken. For 4.

CHICKEN WITH ONIONS (*Pollo con Cebollas*)

Young chicken (3 to 4 pounds)	1
Salt and pepper	To taste
Lemon	1
Onions	½ pound
Fat	3 tablespoons
Sherry wine	1 cup
Small peas	1 cup

Cut chicken in pieces and sprinkle with salt, pepper and lemon juice. Marinate in this for 2 hours.

Cut each onion in four. Melt fat, add chicken and onions, cover and simmer, adding sherry wine gradually. When chicken is tender and onions soft, add the peas. Season well and serve very hot. For 4.

CHICKEN WITH CHESTNUTS CUBAN STYLE
(Pollo con Castañas a la Cubana)

Chestnuts	18
Almonds	18
Hazelnuts	18
Sesame seeds	1 teaspoon
Young chicken (3 to 4 pounds)	1
Salt and pepper	To taste
Lemon	1
Fat	2 tablespoons
Onion	1
Ham	¼ pound
Stock	1 cup
Sherry wine	1 cup

Blanch and toast nuts and sesame seeds, mash or pass through fine chopper. Season chicken pieces with salt, pepper and lemon juice. Brown in hot fat, add minced onion and cubed ham. Cook five minutes, add stock and wine, and when half done add nut paste. Cook until tender and serve very hot. For 4.

MAYAN CHICKEN (*Pollo Estilo Yucatán*)

Spring chickens (1½ pounds)	2
Fat	3 tablespoons
Salt and pepper	To taste
Garlic cloves	2
Toasted bread	1 slice
Powdered cinnamon	⅛ teaspoon
Ground cloves	⅛ teaspoon
Tomato soup	1 cup
Saffron	1 pinch
Vinegar	1 teaspoon
Malaga wine	½ cup
Sesame seeds	1 tablespoon

Split chickens. Open flat, brush with half of the fat, sprinkle with salt and pepper and broil.

Melt rest of the fat, brown garlic cloves, ground toasted bread and spices. Add tomato soup and cook 5 minutes. Add broiled chicken, crushed saffron, vinegar and wine. Cover and cook until chicken is tender and sauce thick. Serve hot with a sprinkling of sesame seeds. For 4.

SPICED CHICKEN WITH SAUSAGES
(*Pollo con Salchichas*)

Young chicken (3 to 4 pounds)	1
Vienna sausages	1 can
Vinegar	¼ cup
Powdered cinnamon	⅛ teaspoon
Ground cloves	⅛ teaspoon
Ground peppercorns	⅛ teaspoon
Butter	3 tablespoons
Water	2 cups
Fried bread slices	2
Salt and pepper	To taste
Sesame seeds	1 tablespoon

Cut chicken in pieces. Slice sausages. Place in saucepan with vinegar and spices. Let stand two or three hours. Place on fire adding butter, water and ground fried bread. Cook until tender, adding more water if necessary. Serve hot with toasted sesame seeds.

The original recipe calls for two Spanish sausages. For 4.

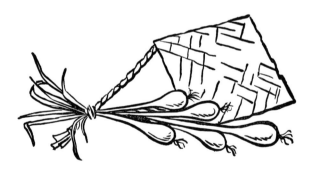

ROASTED STUFFED CHICKEN (*Pollo Relleno*)

Fat	2 tablespoons
Ground pork	2 pounds
Chili powder	1 tablespoon
Chopped tomatoes	1 No. 2 can
Ground cinnamon	⅛ teaspoon
Ground clove	⅛ teaspoon
Almonds (slivered)	18
Raisins	18
Young large chicken (4 to 5 pounds)	1
Salt and pepper	To taste

Melt half of the fat, add pork and chili powder. When meat is brown add chopped tomatoes and spices. Cook until almost dry. Add almonds and soaked raisins. Stuff chicken with mixture, sew, and rub with fat, salt and pepper. Roast in moderate oven, basting with hot water or stock. Serve with a crisp salad. For 4 or 6.

BRAISED CHICKEN (*Estofado de Pollo*)

Large chicken (3 to 4 pounds)	1
Ham	⅛ pound
Garlic	1 clove
Cloves	2 or 3
Small tender onions	2 bunches
Tomato sauce	½ cup
Pepper	To taste
Cinnamon	To taste
Sherry wine	1 cup
Salt	To taste
Almonds	18
Raisins	18

Lard the chicken with small pieces of ham, pieces of garlic and 2 or 3 cloves. Fry whole chicken and when beginning to get brown add onions, tomato sauce, pepper, cinnamon and salt. Cook for a few minutes, then add water, cover pan with a napkin and put lid on tight. Simmer until tender; when half done add wine, almonds and raisins. For 4 or 6.

SPANISH CHICKEN DE LUXE
(*Pollo de Lujo a la España*)

Butter	½ cup
Young chicken (3 to 4 pounds)	1
Salt and pepper	To taste
Stock	1 cup
White wine	1 cup
Curaçao liqueur	1 small glass
Meat extract	¼ teaspoon (optional)
Lemon	1
Cornstarch	1 tablespoon
Oranges	2
Malaga grapes	½ pound

Melt butter in saucepan and add chicken cut in pieces, salt and pepper. When brown add stock. When chicken is half done add wine and Curaçao, meat extract and lemon juice, cornstarch (diluted in a little cold water).

See that it is well seasoned. Cook until sauce is creamy. Garnish with peeled orange slices (or sections with the membrane removed) and peeled grapes. For 4.

CHICKEN WITH ORANGES (*Pollo en Naranja*)

Young chicken (3 to 4 pounds)	1
Fat	3 tablespoons
Salt and pepper	To taste
Ground cinnamon	⅛ teaspoon
Ground clove	⅛ teaspoon
Garlic cloves	2 (optional)
Orange juice	1 cup
Bermuda onion	1
Saffron	1 pinch
Raisins	2 tablespoons
Blanched almonds	2 tablespoons
Capers	1 tablespoon
Water	1 cup

Cut chicken in pieces and fry in hot fat with salt, pepper, cinnamon and cloves, adding garlic cloves if desired. When brown add the orange juice, the sliced onion, saffron, raisins, almonds and capers. Cover and cook gently until chicken is tender. If necessary, add the water. Serve hot with sauce, but remove garlic before serving. Garnish with extra sliced oranges. For 4.

SPANISH STUFFED CHICKEN
(*Pollo Relleno a la Española*)

Ground steak	1½ pounds
Minced ham	¼ pound
Chicken livers	3
Egg	1
Chartreuse liqueur	1 small glass
Salt and pepper	To taste
Young chicken (3 to 4 pounds)	1
Sliced bacon	¼ pound
Garlic cloves	2
Lemon	1

Mix well ground steak, ham, chopped chicken livers, egg, chartreuse, salt and pepper. Stuff chicken with mixture, sew and place in roasting pan with bacon slices and garlic cloves. When brown, add hot water or stock and baste until done. Just before serving time add lemon juice. For 4 or 6.

SPANISH CHICKEN PIE (*Pastel de Pollo*)

Olive oil	1 cup
Young chicken (3 to 4 pounds)	1
Raw ham	½ pound
Garlic	1 clove
Parsley	1 tablespoon
Lemon juice	1 tablespoon
Bay leaf	1
Clove	1
Peppercorns	3
Eggs	5
Salt and pepper	To taste
Pie pastry	

Heat oil with chicken cut in pieces and ham cut in large cubes, minced garlic, parsley, lemon juice and spices. Cook until chicken is tender, adding a little water to prevent scorching.

Beat eggs. Make pastry and line baking dish. Place layers of chicken and beaten eggs, cover with pastry and bake in 350° oven. For 4 or 6.

CHICKEN WITH ALMOND SAUCE

Young chicken (2 pounds)	1
Chicken breast	1
Flour	3 tablespoons
Salt and pepper	To taste
Cooking oil or other shortening	3 tablespoons
Olive oil	3 tablespoons
Large onion	1
Paprika	1 tablespoon
Tomatoes, fresh or canned	2
Almonds	½ cup
Saffron	1 pinch
Stock or water	4 cups
Bay leaf	1
Thyme	1 pinch

Singe and clean chicken. Disjoint and sprinkle with flour, salt and pepper. Fry in hot oil and when it begins to get brown add chopped onion and paprika. When onion is soft, add chopped tomatoes (previously skinned and seeded).

Meanwhile blanch almonds, fry until golden brown and grind with saffron. Add to chicken with stock. Cover and cook until chicken is tender. When almost done add herbs and more salt and pepper if necessary.

If this dish is served at a buffet party, only breasts of

chicken should be used, allowing one for each guest. For 4 or 6.

CHICKEN MADRID   (*Pollo a la Madrileña*)

Carrot	1
Onion	1
Butter	½ cup
Garlic clove	1
Flour	1 tablespoon
Chili powder or paprika	1 tablespoon
Stock	1 cup
Mushrooms	1 pound
Lemon juice	1 tablespoon
Salt	To taste
Young chicken (2 to 3 pounds)	1
Egg yolks	2

Cut carrot in cubes and slice onion. Melt ⅓ of the butter and fry carrot, onion and garlic; add flour, chili powder and stock. Cook 5 minutes and strain. In another pan fry cleaned mushrooms; add lemon juice and add to the sauce. The chicken has been cooked previously in butter on slow fire. When tender add the sauce with mushrooms. Just before serving, dilute egg yolks in a little of the sauce. Serve hot. For 4.

QUAILS WITH QUINCE JELLY
(*Codornices con Jalea de Membrillo*)

Quails	4
Quince peels	2 cups
Brandy	1 cup
Fat	4 tablespoons
Salt and pepper	To taste
Quince jelly	

Two days before serving this dish, place quails in earthen dish with quince peels and brandy. Keep in refrigerator or cool place. Drain from marinade, rub with fat, salt and pepper and roast in hot oven. When brown, add the strained marinade and a little water or stock if necessary. Serve garnished with cress. Serve sauce in sauceboat and quince jelly in glass container. For 4.

TURTLEDOVES IN BROWN SAUCE
(*Tórtolas en Salsa Café*)

Turtledoves (or Rock Cornish game hens, or squabs)	8
Butter	4 tablespoons
Flour	2 tablespoons
Water	2 cups
Sherry wine	1 cup
Salt and pepper	To taste
Almonds	½ cup
Raisins	¼ cup

Clean birds. Melt butter in large saucepan and brown doves, sprinkle with flour and when brown add water. Cover and cook until almost done. Add wine, salt, pepper, blanched almonds and soaked raisins. Cook until birds are tender. Serve hot, garnished with fried croutons and parsley sprigs. For 4.

MARINATED CHICKEN

Young chicken (3 to 4 pounds)	1
Extra breast	1
White wine	2½ cups
Vinegar	½ cup
Bay leaf	1
Thyme	⅛ teaspoon
Marjoram	⅛ teaspoon
Shortening	3 tablespoons
Salt and pepper	To taste
Onion	2 tablespoons

Clean, disjoint chicken and marinate for several hours in wine, vinegar and herbs.

Remove from marinade, dry with towel, sprinkle with salt and pepper and fry until golden brown. In the same shortening, fry chopped onion and when it begins to turn golden, add marinade, cover and cook over slow fire until very tender. For 4 or 6.

CHICKEN VALENTINA

There used to be a small restaurant in Guadalajara owned by a *simpática* woman called Valentina. It became so popular that, in spite of the humbleness of the place, all the best society people used to go there to eat the chicken she prepared. Here is the recipe:

Young chicken (3 to 4 pounds)	1
Onion	1
Celery	1 stalk
Carrot	1
Parsley	1 bunch
Garlic	1 clove
Peppercorns	4
Salt	To taste
Fresh or canned tomatoes	4
Chopped onion	3 tablespoons
Shortening	6 tablespoons
Chicken broth	2 cups
Oregano	¼ teaspoon
Vinegar	1 teaspoon
Sugar	1 teaspoon
Boiled potatoes	2
Romaine, radishes, olives	To garnish

Boil chicken (disjointed) with onion, celery, carrot, parsley, garlic, peppercorns and salt, until tender.

Skin, discard seeds and chop tomatoes. Chop onion.

Heat one half of shortening and fry onion. When it turns golden brown add tomatoes. Simmer and add chicken broth. Cook until it begins to get thick, adding oregano.

Dip pieces of chicken in this sauce and fry in another pan until golden brown. In the same shortening fry peeled and sliced potatoes.

Serve chicken and potatoes immediately, very hot and garnished with romaine leaves, radish roses and olives.

Pass sauce to serve on the chicken. For 4 or 6.

CHICKEN WITH ORANGE SAUCE

Young chicken (3 to 4 pounds)	1
Extra breast	1
Cooking oil	2 tablespoons
Olive oil	2 tablespoons
Fresh or canned tomatoes, peeled, seeded and chopped	4
Sliced onion	1 large
Ground cloves	1 pinch
Ground pepper	⅛ teaspoon
Bay leaf	1
Dried powdered marjoram	1 pinch
Dried powdered thyme	1 pinch
Orange juice	1 cup
Salt	To taste

Singe, clean and cut chicken in pieces. Place in pan with rest of ingredients. Cover well and cook over slow fire until tender. It does not need water. For 4.

CHICKEN WITH POBLANO OR GREEN PEPPERS

Green peppers	1 pound
or	
Canned green peppers cut in strips	1 can
Onions	1 pound
Cooked breasts of chicken	3
Shortening	2 tablespoons
Sour cream	1 cup
Salt	To taste
Grated cheese	1½ cups

If green peppers are used, clean, remove seeds, boil and cut in strips. Slice onion and shred chicken breasts.

Heat shortening and fry sliced onion and peppers. Add shredded chicken and sour cream; salt to taste. Heat well, but do not let the mixture boil. Serve immediately with grated cheese on top.

It is eaten with tortillas. It can also be used as the filling for a pie. For 4 or 6.

FRESH CORN TAMALE

Fresh corn on the cob	12
Lard	4 tablespoons
Flour	3 tablespoons
Baking powder	1 teaspoon
Egg yolks	3
Salt	To taste
Boiled chicken	1
or boiled chicken breasts	3
Mole sauce	3 cups

Cut corn from cob and grind or grate. Heat lard and fry corn, stirring constantly until transparent.

Remove from fire, add flour, baking powder and egg yolks and beat for a few minutes with wooden spoon.

Put half of this mixture in an ovenproof dish or casserole, then chicken without bones and cut in pieces, in the mole sauce. Cover with other half of corn and bake in the oven until cooked. (Insert a long needle to test, like the cakes.)

Tomato sauce may be used instead of the mole sauce.

To make mole sauce, see recipe for Turkey Mole on page 117. For 6 or 8.

BAKED TAMALES

Canned tamales	18
Tomato sauce	2 cups
Sour cream	1 cup
Boiled breast of chicken	1
Grated cheese	1 cup
Salt	To taste

Butter shallow baking dish. Slice tamales and put in layers with sauce, sour cream with a little salt, shredded chicken and grated cheese. Bake in oven until thoroughly heated. Serve at once.

This is a very good dish for a party. For 4 or 6.

RABBIT THE CATALONIAN WAY

Young rabbit	1
Flour	4 tablespoons
Salt and pepper	To taste
Bacon	6 slices
Chopped onion	2 tablespoons
Bay leaf	1
Marjoram and thyme	1 pinch each
Water	2 cups
White wine	2 cups
Almonds (blanched)	8
Shelled piñon nuts	2 tablespoons
Fried bread	1 slice

Disjoint rabbit, wash and dry well. Sprinkle with flour, salt and pepper. Fry bacon until crisp, remove, and in grease left fry rabbit pieces until golden brown. Meanwhile boil rabbit's liver with onion and herbs. Add water and wine to the pan where the rabbit is browning. Cover pan and cook rabbit until tender. Grind almonds, piñon nuts, bread and rabbit's liver. Dilute the paste with a little water and add to rabbit. Let cook until sauce thickens a little.

Serve very hot with steamed potatoes or white rice. For 4.

Vegetables

STUFFED LETTUCE (*Lechuga Rellena*)

Boiled and mashed sweet potatoes	2 cups
Breast of chicken	1
Butter	3 tablespoons
Egg yolks	2
Salt, pepper and nutmeg	To taste
Heads of lettuce	2

Boil, peel and mash sweet potatoes. Pass through a sieve. Fry breast of chicken in butter and pass through a food chopper; mix with the sweet potatoes, egg yolks, salt, pepper and nutmeg.

Clean heads of lettuce, stuff with mixture, tie with string

and cook in salted water, covered and over slow fire. Drain and serve hot. For 6.

SPANISH STUFFED TURNIPS (*Nabos Rellenos*)

Large turnips	12
Ground veal	⅛ pound
Minced ham	⅛ pound
Red pimento	1
Minced onion	1 teaspoon
Minced garlic	1 small clove
Minced parsley	1 teaspoon
Salt and pepper	To taste
Butter	3 tablespoons
Water	½ cup
White wine	½ cup
Egg yolk	1

Peel turnips, cut a slice at round end, hollow and stuff with veal, ham, minced pimento, onion, garlic and parsley. Season well with salt and pepper.

Replace cut-off slice and secure with toothpicks. Fry in butter and place in baking dish. Cover with water and wine. Bake in hot oven. When turnips are soft take sauce, mix with egg yolk, heat well over hot water and pour over the turnips. For 4 or 6.

RAINBOW MOLD (*Molde Arco Iris*)

Potatoes	2 pounds
Eggs	3
Boiled spinach	½ cup
Thick tomato sauce	½ cup
Salt and pepper	To taste

Peel potatoes and steam until very soft. Pass through ricer and season well. Mix with egg whites beaten until stiff. Divide mixture in four parts. To the first add the spinach chopped very fine, to the second part add the thick tomato sauce, to the third the egg yolks and leave the fourth part plain. Butter a mold and place layers of the different colors, dot with butter and bake in oven about 20 minutes. Turn on hot platter and serve plain or with cream sauce. For 6.

LENTILS WITH FRUITS (*Lentejas con Frutas*)

Lentils	1 pound
Fat	2 tablespoons
Tomatoes	3
Minced onion	1 tablespoon
Minced garlic	1 clove (optional)
Pineapple	2 slices
Boiled sweet potato	1
Apple	1
Bananas	2
Salt and pepper	To taste

Boil lentils until tender (they should have some water left).

Melt fat. Add chopped tomatoes, minced onion and garlic. Cook five minutes, add lentils with their water. Cook five minutes more and add the pineapple cut in wedges, the peeled and sliced sweet potato, peeled and sliced apple and sliced bananas. Boil until apple is tender. The mixture should be creamy.

People who dislike the sweet taste may add cubed ham instead of the fruits. For 4 or 6.

LENTILS WITH PORK EARS
(*Lentejas con Orejas de Puerco*)

Lentils	½ pound
Water	To cover
Bacon	3 slices
Pork ears	4
Minced onion	1 tablespoon
Bay leaf	1
Garlic	1 clove (optional)
Clove	1
Salt	To taste

Clean lentils and place in saucepan with water, bacon, pork ears (previously blanched in boiling salted water for five minutes) cut in small pieces, onion, bay leaf, garlic, clove and salt. Boil gently for about 4 hours, adding more water if necessary, but the mixture should be creamy and thick. For 4 or 6.

SWEET POTATO FRITTERS (*Tortitas de Camote*)

Sweet potatoes	2 pounds
Ground steak	½ pound
Fat	1 tablespoon
Chopped tomatoes	½ cup
Minced onion	1 teaspoon
Minced parsley	1 teaspoon
Eggs	3
Salt and pepper	To taste

Boil sweet potatoes, peel and cut in thick slices. Fry meat in hot fat, when brown add the chopped tomatoes, onion and parsley; cook until thick. Put some meat between two slices of sweet potato, sandwich fashion. Dip in flour and then in beaten eggs (white of egg beaten first until stiff and then yolks added). Fry in deep fat. Drain on paper and serve accompanied with tomato sauce.

These fritters can be made the same way using white potatoes. A slice of cheese may be used instead of the meat. For 6 or 8.

CAULIFLOWER FRITTERS (*Tortitas de Coliflor*)

Cauliflower	1
Cheese	¼ pound
Eggs	3
Fat	¼ cup
Minced onion	1 teaspoon
Tomato sauce	3 cups
Minced parsley	1 teaspoon
Chili powder	1 teaspoon
Salt	To taste

Boil cauliflower as usual, uncovered and in salted water. Drain and dry. Divide in medium-size pieces. Place a small slice of cheese in between the flowerets, dip in flour and then in beaten eggs (as for above recipe). Fry in hot fat.

In the fat left, fry onion; when soft, add tomato sauce, parsley and seasonings. Cook ten minutes, add cauliflower fritters and serve at once. For 8.

RAW POTATO FRITTERS (*Tortitas de Papa Cruda*)

Potatoes	1 pound
Eggs	2
Onion	1
Flour	1 teaspoon
Milk	3 tablespoons
Salt and pepper	To taste

Peel potatoes and grate; mix egg yolks with the minced onion and the flour and milk. Then add the egg whites stiffly beaten and season well with salt and pepper. Drop by spoonfuls in the hot fat. Serve at once.

Don't keep mixture after it is ready because it turns dark. For 8.

STRING BEAN FRITTERS
(*Tortitas o Frituras de Ejotes*)

Olive oil	1 tablespoon
Vinegar	1 teaspoon
Mustard	1 teaspoon
Egg	1
Flour	½ cup
Salt and pepper	To taste
Milk	¼ cup
Boiled and diced string beans	2 cups
Fat	½ cup

Mix oil, vinegar and mustard. Add beaten egg, flour, salt and pepper. While beating add milk, little by little. When smooth add string beans. Drop by spoonfuls in the hot fat. For 4 or 6.

NEW POTATOES (*Papitas Nuevas*)

Small new potatoes	1 pound
Butter	½ cup
Egg yolks	3
Stock	1 cup
Salt and pepper	To taste
Prepared mustard	1 tablespoon

Boil potatoes, peel and fry in butter. Add a mixture of the egg yolks with the stock, salt, pepper and mustard. Cook for a few minutes and serve at once. For 4 or 6.

POTATO TORTE (*Torta de Papa*)

Large potatoes	6
Eggs	6
Lemon rind	1 teaspoon
Milk	½ cup
Baking powder	1 teaspoon
Butter	3 tablespoons
Sugar	3 tablespoons

Peel and steam potatoes, pass through ricer and add all the other ingredients. Butter a mold and dust with bread crumbs. Fill with potato mixture and bake in 350° oven for 45 minutes. Serve with sugar or tomato sauce. For 12.

CORN TORTE (*Torta de Elote*)

Corn	2 medium-size cans
Butter	3 tablespoons
Sugar	¼ cup
Cinnamon	1 teaspoon
Eggs	4

Mix corn with melted butter, sugar, cinnamon and yolks. Add egg whites beaten until stiff. Place mixture in buttered mold and bake in 350° oven for 45 minutes, or until set. Serve hot with more sugar as a hot dessert. For 6 or 8.

CALABAZA PUDDING (*Torta de Calabaza*)

Calabacitas are small green squash that grow among the corn. They bear yellow flowers which are very tender. Both calabacitas and flowers are cooked and are very popular in Mexico. If they are tender and small they are cooked whole; later on they are chopped before being cooked.

Boiled and chopped calabacitas or Italian zucchini	4 cups
Butter	2 tablespoons
Minced onion	1 tablespoon
Minced garlic	1 clove (optional)
Tomatoes	1 No. 2 can
Grated Swiss cheese	½ cup
Eggs	4
Salt and pepper	To taste

Chop the boiled calabacitas or, if this special kind is not obtainable, use Italian zucchini. Melt butter and add the onion and garlic; when soft add the chopped tomatoes. Cook 5 minutes and add the squash and the cheese. Remove from fire. Beat egg whites until stiff, add yolks one by one, beating constantly. Add to the mixture. Butter a baking dish and pour in mixture. Cover with dry bread crumbs, dot with butter and bake in hot oven until brown, and egg is set. For 6 or 8.

CALABACITAS PICADAS (*Chopped Calabacitas*)

Green pepper	1
Green corn	2 cobs
Raw chopped calabacitas or squash	4 cups
Chopped tomatoes	4 cups
Minced onion	1 tablespoon
Minced garlic	1 clove (optional)
Salt and pepper	To taste
Olive oil	4 tablespoons
Cream cheese	1 3-ounce package

Clean and boil the green pepper and cut in thin strips. Separate the grains of corn from the cobs and boil for 5 minutes. Oil a casserole and place in alternate layers the squash, tomatoes, onion and garlic, grains of corn, green pepper strips, salt and pepper and oil. Cover and bake in hot oven until squash is done. Serve hot, garnished with crumbled cream cheese. For 6 or 8.

PEAS IN ALMOND SAUCE
(*Chícharos en Salsa de Almendra*)

Fat	2 tablespoons
Almonds	18
Bread slice	1
Young spring onions	1 bunch
Water or stock	2 cups
Peas	1 cup
Salt and pepper	To taste
Minced parsley	1 tablespoon

Melt fat and fry almonds and bread slice. Drain and mash. In the same fat fry whole onions and when golden brown add paste of almonds and bread and some water or stock to make a sauce. Add the peas, season well with salt and pepper and cook until onions are tender. Sprinkle with parsley. For 6.

STRING BEANS WITH YELLOW SAUCE
(*Ejotes en Salsa de Huevo*)

String beans	1 pound
Hard-boiled egg yolks	4
Boiled potato	1
Olive oil	¼ cup
Vinegar	1 teaspoon
Salt and pepper	To taste

Remove strings from beans, dice and boil in salted water. Chop the egg yolks and the boiled potato, adding the oil, vinegar, salt and pepper. Drain water from beans and add sauce. Serve hot. For 6.

STUFFED ARTICHOKES (*Alcachofas Rellenas*)

Young artichokes	12
Butter	¼ cup
Ground veal	¼ pound
Minced ham	¼ pound
Dry bread crumbs	¼ cup
Lemon juice	1 tablespoon
Grated cheese	¼ cup
Hard-boiled egg yolks	4
Stock	½ cup
White wine	½ cup
Salt and pepper	To taste

Remove hard leaves from artichokes, cut off about an inch of the tops and place in water with the juice of one lemon Let stand for one hour. Boil until tender.

Melt butter and fry veal and ham; when brown add bread crumbs and lemon juice. Remove from fire and add grated cheese. Put mixture between leaves of artichokes and place in baking dish. Mash egg yolks and mix with stock and wine. Season well with salt and pepper and pour over artichokes. Bake in moderate oven about 20 minutes. For 6.

SPANISH CABBAGE (*Col a la Española*)

Chick-peas	½ pound
Cabbage	1 head
Fat	3 tablespoons
Minced onion	1 teaspoon
Minced garlic	1 clove
Ham	¼ pound
Chopped tomatoes	2 cups
Salt and pepper	To taste
Red pimentos	2

Soak chick-peas overnight, and next morning boil until skin can be removed. Return to kettle and cook until tender.

In another pan boil cabbage, uncovered, for 10 minutes. Chop.

Melt fat and fry onion and garlic; when soft add minced ham and tomatoes. Cook five minutes, seasoning well with salt and pepper. Add chick-peas and cabbage and cook a little longer. Serve hot, garnished with pimento strips. For 6 or 8.

RED CABBAGE WITH WINE (*Col Morada con Vino*)

Red cabbage	2 heads
Butter	½ cup
Red wine	2 cups
Salt and pepper	To taste

Slice cabbage and place in saucepan with butter. Cook over slow fire for 20 minutes, after which add wine, salt and pepper. Cook gently until very tender. If necessary, add a little stock or hot water. Serve with pork or sausages. For 6.

STUFFED RED PIMENTOS (*Pimientos Rellenos*)

Ham	¼ pound
Vienna sausages	1 small can
Fat	2 tablespoons
Minced onion	1 teaspoon
Rice	¼ pound
Stock	3 cups
Salt and pepper	To taste
Red pimento cups	12
Olive oil	2 tablespoons

Mince ham and slice sausages; fry both in the hot fat, adding minced onion and rice; when golden brown add two cups of the stock and cook until rice is done, seasoning well with salt and pepper. Fill the pimento cups and place in baking dish, pouring over all the oil and one cup of stock. Bake in 375° oven 15 minutes. For 12.

STUFFED GREEN PEPPERS MEXICAN STYLE
(*Chiles Rellenos*)

Fat	2 tablespoons
Ground pork	½ pound
Minced onion	1 teaspoon
Chopped tomatoes	2 cups
Almonds	18
Raisins	18
Salt and pepper	To taste
Green peppers or Poblano peppers	8

Heat fat and fry ground meat until brown, add onion and when soft add tomatoes. Cook until thick; add blanched and chopped almonds, soaked and halved raisins, salt and pepper.

Clean and boil green peppers for 15 minutes. Stuff through slit made to remove seeds and roll in flour.

FOR FRYING

Eggs	3
Deep fat	

Beat egg whites until stiff. Add yolks one by one and continue beating. Dip stuffed peppers in egg mixture and fry in hot fat. Drain on paper. Serve accompanied with a good tomato sauce. For 8.

MEXICAN BEANS (*Frijoles Mexicanos*)

Brown Mexican beans or red kidney beans	½ pound
Lard	1 tablespoon
Onion	1
Salt	To taste

Soak beans overnight in cold water. Next day place in kettle or saucepan with plenty of cold water, lard, onion and salt. Cover with a smaller pan containing water. If beans should become dry in the cooking process, add more warm water from the smaller pan. Let boil constantly until very tender. For 6.

CREAMY BEANS (*Frijoles Espesos*)

Fat	2 tablespoons
Minced onion	1 teaspoon
Flour	1 teaspoon
Beans	Above recipe
Salt	To taste

Melt fat in saucepan (bacon fat is especially good). Add minced onion and when transparent add flour; when it begins to brown add beans with their own liquor, season to taste and cook until creamy.

Minced green pepper, chili powder, and sliced sausages may be added if desired. For 6.

FRIED CRISPY BEANS (*Frijoles Refritos*)

Fat	3 tablespoons
Finely minced onion	1 teaspoon
Cooked beans	Basic recipe
Salt	To taste

Melt fat and add minced onion. When transparent add mashed beans and cook, mashing with fork and stirring constantly until dry. Form a roll that should be dry but crispy and rich on the outside. Serve with grated cheese, and totopos (squares of fried tortillas).

Canned kidney beans may be used, but they are much sweeter in flavor. For 6.

ZUCCHINI FRITTERS

Medium-size Italian squash (zucchini)	4
Cheese	¼ pound (approximately)
Flour	4 tablespoons
Eggs	3
Salt and pepper	To taste

Boil zucchini in salted water until tender but not mushy. Cut in thick slices and put a small slice of cheese between two zucchini slices, sandwich fashion, and sprinkle with flour on both sides.

Beat egg whites until stiff, then add yolks and mix without beating but with a folding motion; add a little salt and pepper.

Dip zucchini sandwiches in beaten egg and fry in hot shortening until golden brown on both sides. Place on brown paper to remove excess grease and serve hot with a good tomato sauce. Or serve without the sauce with the meat course.

Cheese may be Mozzarella or other bland cheese. Cream cheese may be used too. For 6 or 8.

MEXICAN CHICK-PEAS

Chick-peas	½ pound
Bacon	3 slices
Shortening	1 tablespoon
Chopped onion	2 tablespoons
Chopped garlic	1 clove
Tomato sauce	1 cup
Cumin seeds	4
Chili powder	To taste
Hot sausages	2
or vienna sausages	6
Salt	To taste
Minced parsley	2 tablespoons

Wash and soak chick-peas overnight in warm water. Next day boil in plenty of water with salt (it can be done in a pressure cooker).

Render bacon, remove from pan and add shortening. When hot, fry chopped onion and garlic, then tomato sauce and cumin seeds ground in mortar, and chili powder. Let cook for a few minutes, then add chick-peas with their own liquor (skin removed), sliced sausage, and bacon cut in pieces. Season with salt to taste and cook until sauce is thick. Serve very hot, sprinkled with parsley. For 6.

STUFFED ZUCCHINI

Medium-size zucchini	12
Sardines	1 can
Salt and pepper	To taste
Grated cheese	4 tablespoons
French dressing or tomato sauce	
Fresh tomatoes	2
Avocado	1

Boil zucchini in salted water until tender but not mushy. Cut in half lengthwise. Remove white centers and chop, mixing it with the cleaned sardines, cut in small pieces. Season with salt and pepper and fill the cavities of the zucchini. Put grated cheese on top.

If served cold as a salad, pour French dressing over them and garnish with tomato and avocado slices.

If served hot, place in a shallow baking dish with grated cheese on top. Bake in 350° oven until well heated and accompany with a good tomato sauce. For 6.

Salads

TOMATO AND AVOCADO SALAD
(*Ensalada de Aguacate*)

Red firm tomatoes	3
Avocados	3
Small spring onions	1 bunch
French dressing or mayonnaise	½ cup

Slice tomatoes. Peel avocados and slice crosswise. Boil onions. Line glass platter with lettuce leaves, place tomato slices with one avocado slice on top, fill center of avocado with baby onions marinated with French dressing. Pour more French dressing over all or garnish with mayonnaise. For 6.

STUFFED TOMATOES WITH AVOCADO
(*Jitomates o Tomates Rojes Rellenos con Aguacate*)

Small firm tomatoes	6
Avocados	3
Lettuce	2 heads
French dressing	4 tablespoons
Mayonnaise	¼ cup
Chili sauce	1 tablespoon (optional)

Wash and hollow the tomatoes. Peel and mash avocados. Slice very thinly the white part of the lettuce and mix with the mashed avocado, moistening with French dressing and chili sauce. Fill tomatoes with mixture and place on lettuce leaves. Garnish with mayonnaise. Serve at once. For 6.

STUFFED AVOCADOS (*Aguacates Rellenos*)

Avocados	3
Lettuce leaves	6
Boiled potatoes	2
Boiled string beans	1 cup
Celery	1 stalk
Bananas	2
French dressing	¼ cup
Mayonnaise	¼ cup

Peel avocados and cut in halves lengthwise. Place each half on a lettuce leaf on individual plates. Stuff with a mixture of diced potatoes and string beans, chopped celery and bananas, marinated with French dressing. Garnish with mayonnaise. For 6.

STUFFED AVOCADOS (*Aguacates Rellenos*)

Minced celery	½ cup
Blanched almonds	¼ cup
Peeled chopped apples	½ cup
French dressing	3 tablespoons
Avocados	3
Lettuce	1
Mayonnaise	¼ cup

Mix celery with chopped almonds and apples, moisten with French dressing. Peel avocados and cut in halves lengthwise. Place each half on a lettuce leaf and stuff with mixture. Garnish the top with mayonnaise. For 6.

CHICK-PEA SALAD (*Ensalada de Garbanzo*)

Dried chick-peas (or lima beans)	1 cup
Onion	1
Parsley	1 sprig
French dressing	¼ cup
Lettuce	1
Stuffed olives	12
Carrots	3
Hard-boiled eggs	3
Mayonnaise	¼ cup

Lima beans may be used instead of Spanish chick-peas if these are not available.

Soak chick-peas or lima beans overnight. Boil with onion and parsley in salted water. When tender, drain, skin and marinate with French dressing for several hours. Place on lettuce leaves and garnish with olives, sliced carrots and sliced eggs. Place mayonnaise on top. For 6.

SPANISH CHICKEN SALAD (*Ensalada de Pollo*)

Breast of chicken, boiled	1
Red pimentos	2
Small peas	1 cup
Boiled rice	1 cup
French dressing	½ cup
Mustard	1 teaspoon
Minced parsley	1 tablespoon

Cube boiled chicken meat and mix with the other ingredients. Serve cold on lettuce leaves. For 4 or 6.

VEGETABLE SALAD WITH ANCHOVIES
(*Ensalada de Verduras con Anchoas*)

Cooked cubed potatoes	1 cup
Cooked cubed carrots	½ cup
Cooked cubed turnips	½ cup
Cooked diced string beans	½ cup
Cooked peas	½ cup
Mayonnaise	½ cup
Herbs	To taste
Firm tomato	1
Hard-boiled eggs	2
Olives	12
Capers	18
Anchovies	1 can

Mix vegetables with mayonnaise seasoned with herbs. Place on lettuce leaves. Garnish with tomato wedges, sliced hard-boiled eggs, olives, capers and anchovies. For 6 or 8.

SUMMER SALAD (*Ensalada Fresca*)

Green peppers	2
Firm ripe tomatoes	2
Avocados	2
Lettuce	1
French dressing	½ cup
Onion	1

Seed and boil peppers. Chop or cut in strips. Mix with peeled tomatoes cut in wedges and peeled and sliced avocados. Place on crisp leaves of lettuce and pour French dressing over it. Garnish with onion rings. For 4 or 6.

GAZPACHO (*Spanish Tomato Salad*)

This is a very special Spanish salad eaten in the very hot days of summertime. In Andalucía it is eaten with relish by everybody and has several variations.

Mash in a mortar several blanched almonds, one clove of garlic and a bread slice soaked in vinegar. Add plenty of oil until it is reduced to a paste; season with salt. Add this to the salad bowl where we have sliced tomatoes, strips of pimento or green pepper, peeled and sliced cucumbers, minced onion and slices of toasted bread. Add a little water, more oil, vinegar and salt. The dressing should be enough to soak the bread. Place on ice or in refrigerator until serving time.

In some regions instead of the water they add some crushed ice.

CAULIFLOWER SALAD (*Ensalada de Coliflor*)

Cauliflower	1
French dressing	½ cup
Blanched almonds	½ cup
Avocados	4
Salt and pepper	To taste
Nutmeg	To taste
Lettuce	1
Small red radishes	1 bunch

Boil cauliflower and soak with French dressing. Pound blanched almonds in mortar and mix with the mashed avocados. Season the paste with salt, pepper and nutmeg. Drain cauliflower and place on lettuce leaves, cover with avocado paste, and garnish with radish roses. For 8 or 10.

STUFFED GREEN PEPPERS (*Chiles Rellenos Fríos*)

Green peppers or Poblano peppers	6
French dressing	¼ cup
Avocados	4
Olive oil	2 tablespoons
Grated Swiss cheese	½ cup
Salt and pepper	To taste
Corn	1 can
Radish roses	12

Clean and boil peppers until tender. Discard seeds and marinate with French dressing. Peel avocados and mash with fork, mix with oil and cheese and season with salt and pepper.

Stuff peppers with corn and place on platter. Cover with avocado paste, garnish with radishes. Serve cold. For 6.

Desserts

ROYAL EGGS (*Huevos Reales*)

Egg yolks	9
Butter	1 tablespoon
Sugar	1 cup
Water	½ cup
Cinnamon	1 stick
Sherry wine	¼ cup
Almonds	18
Raisins	18

Beat egg yolks until thick and lemon-colored. Place in buttered plain mold with tight cover. Steam over boiling water until set. Make a syrup with sugar, water and cinnamon. When thick, remove from fire and add wine.

Slice custard and place slices on crystal platter. Cover with syrup. Garnish, inserting pieces of blanched almonds and raisins in the custard. For 6 or 8.

COCONUT DESSERT (*Cocada*)

Milk	2½	cups
Sugar	2	cups
Moist coconut	1	can
Egg yolks	5	
Sherry wine	¼	cup (optional)
Almonds	12	

Place milk and sugar in a saucepan and cook until mixture begins to get thick, add coconut and cook, stirring constantly, 10 minutes longer. Remove from fire, cool and add beaten egg yolks. Place on fire again and cook until thick. Add sherry if desired. Pour into a casserole, garnish with blanched halved almonds and place under broiler to brown. For 6.

MILK AND SWEET POTATO DESSERT
(*Dulce de Camote*)

Milk	1	quart
Sugar	1	pound
Cinnamon	1	stick
Boiled and mashed sweet potatoes	2	cups
Sherry wine	½	cup

Place milk with the sugar and cinnamon on the fire. When it begins to boil add the sweet potatoes, stirring continuously until thick.

Remove from fire and add the wine. Pour on platter and

sprinkle with powdered cinnamon. Or serve in small individual plates garnished with whipped cream and a cherry. For 6.

SWEET POTATO AND PINEAPPLE DESSERT
(*Dulce de Camote y Piña*)

Sweet potatoes	1 pound
Pineapple juice	2 cups
Sugar	1 cup

Boil sweet potatoes, mash and pass through sieve. Place juice with sugar on fire; when mixture starts to get thick add mashed sweet potatoes and cook 10 minutes longer, stirring constantly. Remove from fire, cool slightly and pour on platter sprinkling with powdered cinnamon. For 6.

WHITE CUSTARD (*Flan de Claras*)

Milk	1 quart
Cinnamon	1 stick
Sugar	¼ pound
Almonds	½ pound
Egg whites	8

Scald milk with cinnamon; add sugar and almonds (blanched and pounded in mortar). Cook until thick, cool slightly and add egg whites beaten until stiff. Pour in buttered plain mold and bake like a custard. Turn on crystal platter. For 6.

BANANA DESSERT (*Dulce de Plátano*)

Sugar	2 cups
Water	¾ cup
Mashed bananas	2 cups
Sponge cake	
Sherry	
Almonds	
Raisins	

Make a syrup with the sugar and water, add the bananas and cook until thick. Take a platter and place layers of sponge cake slices, dipped in wine, and banana paste. Garnish the top with almonds and raisins. For 8.

BREAD AND WINE DESSERT
(*Dulce de Pan y Huevo*)

Stale bread	¼ loaf
Sugar	1 pound
Egg yolks	5
Sherry	½ cup

Cube the bread. Boil the sugar with a little water and when it starts to get thick, remove from fire and add the beaten egg yolks and the cubed bread. Return to fire and cook gently until the bread is transparent. Add the wine. Serve in small glass dishes. For 6.

CHICK-PEA AND PINEAPPLE DESSERT
(*Dulce de Garbanzo y Piña*)

Spanish chick-peas	1 cup
Molasses	½ cup
Water	1 cup
Pineapple juice	½ cup
Pineapple	1 cup

Soak chick-peas overnight. Next day boil until very tender. Mix molasses with water and pineapple juice. When it begins to boil, add skinned chick-peas and pineapple cut in wedges. Cook until very thick.

This is a typical dessert from Oaxaca, one of Mexico's most interesting states. For 6.

PARADISE DESSERT (*Dulce Paraíso*)

Sugar	½ cup
Water	½ cup
Liqueur	1 small glass
Ladyfingers	12
Sugar	¾ cup
Milk	1 pint
Cornstarch	2 tablespoons
Eggs	3
Almonds	¼ pound

Boil sugar (½ cup) and water 10 minutes. Remove from fire and add liqueur (any at hand). Place ladyfingers on glass platter and cover with syrup.

Place ¾ cup of sugar with milk on fire; add cornstarch diluted with a little cold milk, and beaten eggs. Cook gently, stirring constantly.

After a few minutes add blanched almonds reduced to paste in mortar. When thick remove from fire, cool slightly and pour on ladyfingers. Sprinkle with powdered cinnamon and chill. For 6.

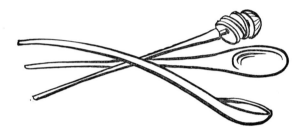

CONVENT'S CUSTARD (*Flan del Convento*)

Milk	1 pint
Cinnamon	1 stick
Cornstarch	¼ cup
Eggs	4
Sugar	½ cup
Ladyfingers	1 dozen

FOR CARAMEL SAUCE

Sugar	4 tablespoons
Water	4 tablespoons

Scald milk with cinnamon. Remove cinnamon and cool milk. Add cornstarch diluted in a half cup of milk or water. Beat eggs with sugar and add little by little to milk.

Place 4 tablespoons sugar in frying pan and when dark brown add water. Remove and pour in plain mold to line bottom. Then place alternate layers of ladyfingers and mixture of eggs and milk. Cover tightly and bake like any other custard. Chill in mold several hours and turn on platter. For 6.

FRIED CREAM (*Crema Frita*)

Milk	1 cup
Cinnamon	1 stick
Eggs	4
Rice flour	1½ ounces
Sugar	½ cup
Bread flour	¼ cup
Dry bread crumbs	½ cup
Butter for frying	

Scald milk with cinnamon. In a saucepan mix 3 egg yolks with rice flour and sugar; add milk, beating well. Place mixture on fire and cook gently, stirring constantly until very thick. Pour in buttered or oiled tray. Chill. Cut in squares, dip in flour, then in beaten egg and bread crumbs and fry in hot butter. Serve hot on platter lined with napkin. Syrup, honey or marmalade may accompany this dish. For 6.

APPLE AND ALMOND PUDDING
(*Budín de Manzana y Almendra*)

Tart apples	12
Stale ladyfingers	5
Almonds	¼ pound
Butter	¼ cup
Sugar	¾ cup
Powdered cinnamon	To taste
Raisins	½ cup

Peel apples and slice thinly. Butter a baking dish and dust with crumbled ladyfingers. Blanch almonds and pound in mortar until reduced to paste. Place alternate layers of apples, bits of almond paste, bits of butter, sugar, powdered cinnamon, raisins and crumbled ladyfingers.

Bake in 325° oven until apples are done. Serve hot. For 6.

LITTLE CUPS (*Copitas*)

Almonds or hazelnuts	¼ **pound**
Sugar	1½ **cups**
Water	⅓ **cup**
Egg yolks	**8**
Vanilla	**1 teaspoon**
Powdered cinnamon	

Blanch almonds, toast until golden brown and pound in mortar. Boil sugar with water 2 or 3 minutes. Remove from fire, cool and add egg yolks one by one, beating well. Place on fire, stirring constantly with clockwise movement; when it begins to get thick, remove from fire and beat well. Add almonds and vanilla and place in glass cups sprinkled with powdered cinnamon. For 6.

DARK BREAD PUDDING (*Capirotada*)

(Special Dish from Guadalajara)

Stale bread	½ loaf
Butter	½ cup
Molasses	1 cup
Water	1 cup
Lemon	1
Cinnamon	⅛ teaspoon
Anise seed	1 teaspoon
Cream cheese	1 3-ounce package
Soaked raisins	¼ cup
Malaga wine	¼ cup

Slice bread and cut each slice in small squares; fry in butter.
Place in saucepan molasses, water, lemon juice, cinnamon
and anise seed. Cook 5 minutes and strain.

In a baking dish place layers of bread, crumbled cheese,
raisins and molasses mixture. Bake in moderate oven 45
minutes. When out of the oven pour wine over it. Serve
hot. For 6.

BANANAS WITH CREAM (*Plátanos con Crema*)

Bananas	6
Butter	¼ pound
Sherry wine	½ cup
Sugar	1 cup
Cream	1 cup
Vanilla	½ teaspoon

Peel bananas, slice lengthwise and fry in butter. Place in
serving platter, pouring sherry wine over them and sprinkle
with half of the sugar.

Whip cream and add vanilla and remaining sugar. Cover bananas, serve cold. For 6.

PEACH AND CREAM GELATIN

Freestone peaches without the stones	2 pounds
Powdered sugar	1 cup
Unflavored gelatin	1½ envelopes
Whipping cream	1 cup
Granulated sugar	1 cup
Water	2 cups
Lemon juice	½ teaspoon

Peel peaches and mash half of them, adding the powdered sugar and the gelatin, previously soaked in ½ cup of cold water and melted in double boiler. Do this as quickly as possible to avoid the darkening of the peaches. Add the whipped cream. Mix well and pour into a wet mold. Place in refrigerator to set.

In a saucepan put granulated sugar and water. When boiling point is reached, add lemon juice and let boil for five minutes. Add the other half of the peaches, peeled and cut in pieces. Let cook until thick, almost like a jam.

At serving time, wet crystal platter. Separate gelatin from sides of mold (only the top) and dip for a few seconds in lukewarm water. Turn on the platter. If not well centered it can be straightened because the platter is wet. Put the peach jam in the center.

While working with the raw peaches, keep in water with a little salt to avoid their darkening. For 6.

CREAM AND PRUNE GELATIN

Milk	2 cups
Sugar	1 cup
Orange	1
Eggs	3
Unflavored gelatin	2 envelopes
Vanilla	¼ teaspoon
Whipping cream	1 cup
Cooked prunes	2 cups
Sugar	½ cup

Pit the prunes.

Put milk in a saucepan with the 1 cup of sugar and the peel of the orange cut in small pieces. Let it come to boil and strain. When lukewarm add yolks diluted in a little milk, stirring to avoid curdling. Place on fire again and cook until thick, always stirring. Add the gelatin (previously soaked in half a cup of water). Remove from fire and add vanilla.

When cold and starting to thicken, add the cream without whipping if a smooth gelatin is desired, and whipped if it is wanted very light and spongy; in this case the beaten egg whites may be added too. It is very good both ways. Put in a wet mold, in the refrigerator.

Place pitted prunes cut in pieces with sugar and orange juice on the fire and cook until thick, almost like a jam.

Unmold the gelatin as usual, and put the prune jam in the center. For 6.

MANGO DELIGHT

Sugar	¾ cup
Eggs	4
Milk	2 cups
Cornstarch	1 tablespoon
Water	¼ cup
Lemon	1
Mangoes	1 can
Sugar for the meringue	6 tablespoons
Vanilla	½ teaspoon

Mix well sugar, yolks and milk. Add cornstarch mixed with cold water and cook in a double boiler, on a very slow fire and stirring constantly until thick. Add a little lemon juice and rind to taste.

Strain mango slices and put in a casserole. Cover with the cold custard.

Beat 3 of the egg whites with 1 teaspoon cold water and beat until stiff but not dry. Add sugar very little at a time, beating all the time, and add vanilla if desired. Cover the custard with this meringue and place the dish in a slow oven (300°) for 15 minutes or until light brown on top. Serve cold. For 6.

ICE CREAMS AND ICES
(Helados y Nieves)

ICE CREAM is a favorite dessert in Spain as well as in Mexico — vanilla, chocolate, coffee, strawberry, etc. — but as they are so well known in the United States I have chosen just a few that are less known.

HAZELNUT ICE CREAM (*Helado de Avellana*)

Milk	1½ quarts
Sugar	2 cups
Egg yolks	10
Cream	1 pint
Hazelnuts	½ pound
Sugar	½ pound

Scald milk with sugar, cool and add the well-beaten egg yolks and the whipped cream.

Caramelize the ½ pound of sugar with the nuts and pour on greased plate. When cold, pound coarsely and add to the cream. Freeze.

MANGO ICE CREAM (*Helado de Mango*)

Fresh mango pulp	1 pound
Whipped cream	2 cups
Sugar	¼ cup

Mix ingredients and freeze. It is delicious.

RED WINE ICE (*Nieve de Vino Tinto*)

Sugar	1½ cups
Water	½ cup
Carbonated water	1 quart
Red wine	1 cup
Lemon	1

Boil sugar and water for 5 minutes, strain through damp cloth and cool. Add carbonated water, wine and lemon juice. Freeze.

WATERMELON ICE (*Helado de Melón*)

Watermelon juice	1 quart
Sugar	1¼ cups
Brandy	6 teaspoons
Lemon juice	1 tablespoon

Peel off rind of watermelon and pass through sieve to obtain juice. Mix with other ingredients and freeze.

CANDIES (*Bombones*)

CHOCOLATE BALLS (*Bolitas de Chocolate*)

Chocolate	6 squares
White Karo	½ cup
Liqueur	To taste
Almonds	¼ pound

Grind chocolate. Mix with blanched and chopped almonds, syrup and liqueur so as to form a paste easy to handle. Shape into balls the size of a marble. Roll in sugar.

COFFEE AND MILK CARAMELS
(*Caramelos de Café con Leche*)

Sugar	½ pound
Butter	½ cup
White wine	1 small glass
Strong coffee	1 cup
Cream	1 cup

Put saucepan over fire with sugar, butter and wine. Cook for ten minutes, stirring constantly. Add coffee and cream and continue cooking and stirring until it reaches the hard-ball consistency. Pour in buttered square tray and when cool cut in squares. When cold wrap in waxed paper and keep in glass jar.

CARAMELIZED YOLKS (*Yemitas*)

Egg yolks	12
Sugar	½ pound
White Karo	2 cups

Beat egg yolks and add sugar, mixing very well. Place mixture in saucepan and cook, stirring constantly until it starts to boil. When cold, form balls, dusting hands with sugar. Let these balls stand for three or four hours. Prepare a thick syrup, not allowing it to reach caramel stage, and dip egg balls, removing them with two forks. Drain on wire sieve. They are eaten when dry.

ALMOND EGGS (*Huevitos de Almendra*)

Water	2 cups
Sugar	1 pound
Almonds	½ pound
Egg yolks	8
Butter	1 tablespoon
Cream	1 tablespoon

Place water and sugar in saucepan. When it begins to thicken, add almonds (blanched and pounded in mortar until reduced to a fine paste), and then well-beaten egg yolks. Cook until very thick, stirring constantly, add butter and cream. Remove from fire and pour on china dish. Let stand overnight and next morning form balls the size of a bird's egg. Roll in a mixture of sugar and powdered cinnamon and wrap in fringed squares of colored tissue paper — half pink and half white for instance.

ALMOND AND NUT MACAROONS
(*Camaroncitos de Almendra*)

Almonds	¼ pound
Nuts	¼ pound
Egg yolks	2
Baking powder	1 teaspoon
Stale bread crumbs	2 teaspoons
Sugar	1 cup
Cinnamon	To taste

Pass almonds and nuts (without blanching) through fine food chopper. Mix with egg yolks, baking powder, crumbs, sugar and cinnamon to form a paste. Shape as crescents and place on floured tin and bake in moderate oven. While still warm, dip in powdered sugar.

Pastry and Cakes

CARROT CAKE (*Torta de Zanahoria*)

Sugar	1¼	cups
Eggs	5	
Grated carrots	2	cups
Blanched almonds	½	pound
Cornstarch	3	tablespoons
Lemon	1	
Kirsch	2	tablespoons

Cream sugar and egg yolks. Add grated carrots, ground almonds and cornstarch, then rind, juice of lemon, kirsch, and finally egg whites beaten until stiff. Butter mold and sprinkle with flour. Pour mixture and bake in moderate oven.

SPANISH CHICK-PEA CAKE (*Torta de Garbanzo*)

Spanish chick-peas	¾ pound
Egg yolks	6
Cinnamon	⅛ teaspoon
Sugar	¾ pound
Egg whites	4
Cream	½ cup
Toasted dry bread crumbs	3 tablespoons

Soak chick-peas in cold water 6 hours. Boil until tender. Skin and leave overnight on clean cloth to dry. Next day pass through fine food chopper or pound in mortar until reduced to a paste. Sift.

Beat egg yolks with cinnamon and sugar until thick. Beat egg whites until stiff and mix with egg yolks, then add chick-pea paste, mixing carefully with a wooden spatula, and lastly add whipped cream. Butter plain mold and sprinkle with dry toasted bread crumbs. Bake in moderate oven about one hour. Cool in mold for 20 minutes and turn out. Sprinkle with more powdered sugar mixed with cinnamon.

MELON CAKE (*Torta de Melón*)

Cantaloupe juice	1 cup
Sugar	1⅓ cups
Egg yolks	12
Cornstarch	2½ cups
Butter	½ cup
Egg whites	6

Place in saucepan melon juice, sugar and egg yolks, beating with a wire whisk until thick. Add sifted cornstarch little by little, mixing well with a wooden spatula, then add melted cool butter and finally egg whites beaten until stiff. Butter mold, line with paper and fill mold ⅔ full with batter. Place immediately in moderate oven and bake about 45 minutes.

CANTALOUPE MARMALADE (*Mermelada de Melón*)

Cantaloupe meat	½ pound
Sugar	¼ pound
Rum	2 tablespoons

Cut cantaloupe meat in cubes and place in pan with sugar. Cook, stirring until thick. Remove from fire and add rum. Cool. Turn into crystal container.
Serve a slice of cake with some of the marmalade.

MANTECADAS DE ASTORGA
(*Little Cakes in Paper Cases*)

Flour	2½ cups
Sugar	1¼ cups
Butter	1½ cups
Eggs	6

Sift the flour three times. Mix sugar and butter and beat until creamy. Add eggs one by one and continue beating after each addition until the dough is perfectly smooth and creamy. Make or buy 25 little paper cases and fill them with the dough, sprinkling the top with granulated sugar. Bake at 375° for about 15 minutes.

CHAMPURRADAS GUATEMALTECAS
(*Little Guatemala Cakes*)

Flour	5 cups
Baking soda	¼ teaspoon
Shortening	1½ cups
Eggs	3
Sugar	1¼ cups
Anise extract	2 tablespoons
Milk	As needed
Sesame seeds	To taste

Sift flour and baking soda three times. Make a hole in the flour on the pastry board and place shortening, eggs, sugar and anise extract in the center. Mix with hands without kneading and adding a little milk only if necessary to make the dough. Roll on floured board about ¼ inch thick. Cut with diamond-shaped cutter, brush with egg, sprinkle with sesame seeds and bake.

POLVORONES DE NARANJA (*Orange Sand Tarts*)

Shortening	1½ cups
Powdered sugar	1 cup
Egg yolks	3
Rind of 1 orange	
Juice of 2 oranges	
Flour	5 cups
Baking soda	1 teaspoon

Cream shortening and sugar. Add yolks one by one, then add the rind and juice of the oranges. Sift flour and baking soda three times and add to mixture. Roll on floured board about ½ inch thick. Cut with round cutter and bake in hot oven from 8 to 10 minutes. Wrap in tissue paper and cut fringe at ends. They are very rich.

There is a large variety of *bizcochos* (cakes) sold in bakeries and distributed by peddlers in big baskets, before breakfast time. Most of them are made with compressed yeast. Here are some:

OJALDRAS (*Little Puff Paste Cakes*)

Flour	3 cups
Yeast	1 cake
Sugar	½ cup
Salt	½ teaspoon
Shortening	¾ cup
Milk	¼ cup
Water	½ teaspoon

Take ½ cup of flour and mix with the yeast dissolved in 3 tablespoons of lukewarm water. Make a soft dough. Let stand in warm place from 10 to 15 minutes, or until double in bulk.

Sift the rest of the flour with sugar and salt and make a hole in the flour. Place in the center half of the shortening, the yeast dough, milk and water. Make a dough, beating it against the board until it makes bubbles. Let stand from 3 to 4 hours.

Take dough and add the other half of the shortening. Beat well so that it mixes thoroughly. Divide in 20 portions and form balls. Place on baking sheet and let stand in warm place until double in bulk. Brush with melted shortening and bake in hot oven for about 20 minutes. Heat before serving.

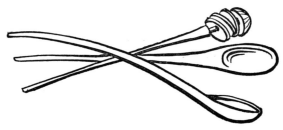

VOLCANES (*Volcanos*)

Flour	3 cups
Yeast	1 cake
Salt	⅛ teaspoon
Lard	¼ cup
Butter	⅛ cup
Sugar	⅓ cup
Eggs	3

FINE PASTE

Flour	½ cup
Sugar	¼ cup
Shortening	¼ cup
Egg yolk	1

Take ¼ cup of flour and mix with the yeast dissolved in 3 tablespoons of lukewarm water. Make a soft dough. Let stand in warm place until double in bulk.

Sift remainder of flour with the salt three times; make a hole in the flour. Put the other ingredients in the center, together with the yeast dough. Mix well with hands, and beat against the board until it makes bubbles and does not stick any more. Place in greased pan, brush with a little shortening, cover with napkin and let stand in warm place several hours until double in bulk. Divide the dough in 20 portions and form balls with the hands. Place on baking sheets. Place on top of each a crown of fine paste, which you must flatten a little with your hand. Brush with egg, sprinkle with some sugar and bake from 12 to 15 minutes.

To make fine paste, mix all the ingredients without handling much.

Mexican Festivals

CHRISTMAS

(*Navidad*)

CHRISTMAS is undoubtedly the principal and gayest of all festivals. The celebrations last nine days and are called the *posadas* (inns) in remembrance of the search for shelter of the Blessed Mother, when arriving in Bethlehem.

The markets of the city are filled with vendors of *piñatas*, big clay vessels adorned on the outside with tissue or crepe paper in the most fantastic way. Some imitate flowers, others animals, airplanes or even persons (a clown for instance). The vessel is concealed by the cardboard forming the figure and by colored paper, and it is filled with fruits, candy and even unbreakable small toys. (Tradition says that piñatas were invented by the Spanish missionaries in order to attract and amuse Indians and convert them to Christianity.)

There are also mounds of fruits, especially oranges, limes, peanuts, sugar cane cut in pieces, and other tropical fruits.

The house where the posada is going to take place is adorned with pine branches, moss, paper lanterns, etc.

The piñata is hung in the patio (yard) or garden.

When the guests arrive, they are given small colored candles and the procession starts. Everybody sings and prays for about thirty minutes, after which they go to the yard where the piñata is hung.

The children, and sometimes the grownups too, take turns in being blindfolded and, with a cane or stick, try to break the piñata. The first attempts, of course, are never successful and at least one hour is spent among the merry shoutings, jokes, etc., of the gathering.

Most of the time firecrackers and other fireworks are set off while the people try to break the piñata.

At last a lucky person breaks it and all the children throw themselves to the ground (usually covered with a carpet) trying to get as much fruit as possible.

The grown-up people get fruits too, but from big baskets that are passed around, as well as large trays with candy, toys and favors.

Then the music starts playing for the young folks to dance. A cold buffet supper is served around midnight.

For Christmas Eve and Christmas Day we have the tree, the presents, the coming of Santa Claus with toys for the children, and many other customs that have probably come from other countries but that feel quite at home in Mexico now.

The big dinner, of course, is something to be remembered. Turkey is the central feature, either roasted or in mole, and around it are many other fine dishes. I am giving here some recipes of special Christmas delicacies.

MEXICAN CHRISTMAS SALAD
(*Ensalada de Nochebuena*)

Romaine	1	
Beets	3	
Carrots	4	
Oranges	3	
Sweet limes	3	
Apples	3	
Bananas	3	
French dressing	3	tablespoons
Sugar	1	tablespoon
Peanuts	1	cup
Salt	1	dash
Jicamas	2	

Wash and slice romaine very fine. Boil, scrape and slice beets and carrots. Peel and slice oranges, limes, apples, and bananas. Mix everything. Pour French dressing and sugar over it and mix again. Sprinkle with peanuts. Some people add sliced radishes but personally I dislike the taste. The only ingredient that cannot be obtained in the United States is the *jicama,* a root somewhat resembling the turnip, but sweet and very watery, that is eaten raw. For 12.

Besides the main dessert we have for Christmas many special cookies, candies, etc. The most popular are the Spanish Turrones and the Marrons Glacés (candied glacéd chestnuts).

TURRON DE ALICANTE

Sugar	½ pound
Honey	½ pound
Egg whites	5
Blanched and toasted almonds	1 pound
Cubed sugar	1 cup
Orange or lemon water	

Mix the granulated sugar with the honey, place on fire and cook until it starts to thicken.

Beat the egg whites until stiff and add to the mixture. Stir continuously until soft crack point. Add the dry almonds and the cubed sugar moistened with the lemon or orange water. Mix well again and when it reaches the hard crack point place in wooden box or in square mold lined with waxed paper.

TURRON DE JIJONA

Granulated sugar	½ pound
Honey	½ pound
Blanched and toasted almonds	½ pound
Toasted hazelnuts	½ pound
Egg whites	5

Mix sugar and honey and place on fire. When mixture starts to get thick add a mixture of the nuts (pound in mortar) and stiffly beaten egg whites. Stir constantly and when very thick remove from fire and pour mixture in square molds lined with waxed paper.

TURRON DE YEMA

Almonds	1 pound
Confectioners' sugar	1 pound
Egg yolks	8
Lemon rind	1 tablespoon
Powdered cinnamon	1 tablespoon

Blanch almonds and pound well in mortar. Mix well with powdered sugar and with egg yolks, then add lemon rind and cinnamon. Work for about 30 minutes. Line mold with waxed paper and fill with mixture, pressing with hands, and place weight on top for several hours. No fire needed.

All these turrones keep well for weeks. Only a little may be eaten at a time as they are quite rich but delicious.

MARRONS GLACES (*Candied Chestnuts*)

Choose the biggest chestnuts you can find. Remove the first skin and place in pan with cold water. Heat on fire and remove when second skin is loose and easily removed.

Prepare a syrup of sugar and water and when it reaches the soft ball test add the chestnuts and boil for two or three minutes. Drain. Next day repeat same operation in the same syrup, and continue to repeat for a few days until chestnuts are soft. Drain from syrup, dry and wrap in aluminum foil.

RADISH NIGHT

(*Noche de Rábanos*)

IN OAXACA there is a very interesting celebration on Christmas Eve called Radish Night.

Big red radishes are plentiful during this season and people cut them in fancy shapes and soak them in water overnight. Next day they look like large fantastic flowers, with which they trim small stands or restaurants around the main garden or plaza (square).

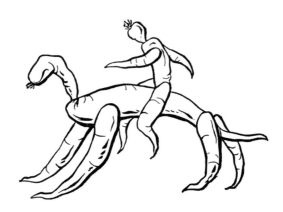

Vendors have been saving cracked or irregular Oaxaca dishes all the year, and on Radish Night they sell buñuelos in these dishes. The fun consists in eating the buñuelos and then breaking the dishes. Around midnight, the square is filled with piles of broken dishes. The main food of course is the

BUNUELOS (Fritters)

Flour	1½ pounds
Salt	½ teaspoon
Baking powder	1 teaspoon
Eggs	4
Shortening	½ cup
Water	As necessary

Sift the flour three times with the salt and baking powder. Mix with the eggs, and shortening and add a little water, if necessary, to make a soft dough. Knead it until it does not stick on the board. Brush with a little shortening and let stand for one hour. Take pieces the size of a walnut and roll paper-thin.

Fry in hot fat. Serve with molasses or maple syrup.

JANUARY 6TH

(The Coming of the Kings)
(*Fiesta de los Santos Reyes*)

ALTHOUGH many children receive their presents from Santa Claus, there are still many families who keep the old Spanish tradition of having their children place their shoes at windows to get the toys from the three kings passing by. (Others are fortunate enough to receive toys on both occasions.)

There is a very interesting celebration on this date. A party is prepared with nice good things to eat, especially a big cake called The King's Ring. A tiny china doll (or a big dry lima bean) is hidden in the dough. The person who finds it in his piece of cake is crowned king or queen and has the right of choosing a partner for the evening — but has also the obligation of giving another party to which all the people present are invited. Sometimes it happens that the person who gets the doll or bean swallows it, in order to avoid the responsibility of giving the party.

If the party is given by a club it changes slightly. Sometimes they give small cake rings (enough for two people). The girls are supposed to cut their rings and give half to their partners. Only one of the rings has the doll, and the boy and girl who get it are crowned king and queen for the evening, and a beautiful present is given to the lucky girl.

Here is the recipe for the cake:

ROSCA DE REYES

Pastry flour	5 cups
Yeast	1 ounce
Whole eggs	4
Egg yolks	8
Salt	⅓ teaspoon
Sugar	¾ cup
Orange blossom water	1 tablespoon
Butter	1¼ cups
Finely shredded citron	¼ pound
Currants	¼ pound

Take 1½ cups of flour and mix it with the yeast and 3

tablespoons of lukewarm water. Make a soft dough and leave it for about 10 or 15 minutes in a warm place. When double in bulk it is ready.

Form a circle with the sifted flour and place in the center of the dough made with the yeast, the eggs, salt, sugar and orange blossom water and half of the butter. Mix all very well, working and beating the dough well. Add the rest of the butter and work until very smooth. Place in a pan and grease slightly and cover with napkin. Let rise until double in bulk (it takes several hours in a warm place). Knead again and roll on floured board to form a strip of about 10 inches wide and 35 inches long. Place citron and currants and roll lengthwise, join both ends firmly and place on greased oven sheet, making a round or oval shape. Let rise again to double in bulk (about an hour and a half). Brush with beaten egg and granulated sugar. Garnish with candied cherries and strips of candied fig or angelica, pasting them with a little thick syrup. Place in hot oven about 10 minutes, then reduce the temperature to moderate and bake from 30 to 40 minutes.

This recipe makes a large ring; half of the amount may be used. Instead of the orange blossom water, rind of one orange and juice of a half may be used.

VIERNES DE DOLORES

(Friday of the Seven Sorrows)

JUST A WEEK before Good Friday, Mexican people celebrate "The Sorrows of Our Lady" with a grand festival at Xochimilco or The Sunken Garden. This place is also called the Mexican Venice because there are many canals among artificial isles where marvelous flowers grow all year round. It is really a miracle of green and a symphony of colors.

It is less than an hour's ride from Mexico City and people go there by trolley cars and automobiles. Immediately they go toward the lake. The sight is fantastic: the sun is rising, the lake is crowded with Mexican gondolas or canoes decorated with flowers and equipped with benches or miniature chairs. Indians are ready to receive people with crowns of flowers for their heads and bunches of carnations for the floral battle. Gay groups get into the canoes and the trip commences through the famous *chinampas*. In the different isles there are stands for important people who will act as judges in the contests that will take place. There are prizes for the best decorated canoe, the best couple of typical dancers, the best guitar player, the best singer, the best typical costume, etc.

Finally the canoes reach Santa Anita, another small village where, in the cafés and restaurants, people will take the typical breakfast of enchiladas or hot tamales with Champurrado.

CHAMPURRADO

Milk	1¼ cups
Cinnamon	1 small piece
Grated chocolate	2 tablespoons
Cornstarch	1 tablespoon
Sugar	To taste

Scald milk with cinnamon, grated chocolate, and cornstarch (diluted in a little cold milk or water) and sugar to taste. Cook until creamy. Serve hot in cups.

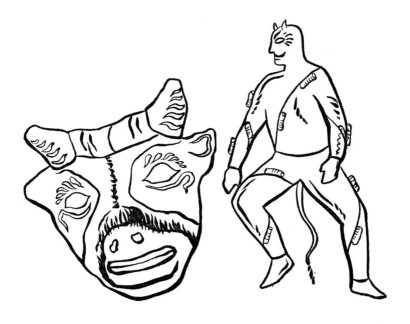

HOLY WEEK

(*Semana Santa*)

DURING Holy Week several sections of the city have stands where they sell *matracas*, typical china, candies, and special cardboard figures representing Judas with firecrackers attached. There are some gigantic ones burned in the streets in some of the suburbs and smaller ones burned in the houses by children.

The typical dishes are Revoltijo (mixture), made with a leafy vegetable cooked in mole, with shrimp cakes. Also Dry Cod Viscay (see FISH section of this book) and Empanadas.

EMPANADAS (*Baked Turnovers*)

Flour	3 cups
Sugar	2 tablespoons
Salt	¼ teaspoon
Shortening	½ cup
Egg	1
Milk	½ cup

Sift flour three times with sugar and salt. Add shortening and beaten egg, then milk, little by little. Mix well and knead to form a soft, smooth dough. Roll thin and cut in rounds. Place a little of the filling in the center of each round and fold, moistening edges together and pressing well. Brush with beaten egg and bake for ten minutes at 450°, then reduce to 350° for remaining time to cook through.

The filling consists of cooked fish but here is another filling that is very good too:

Bermuda onions	3
Oil	3 tablespoons
Lard	2 tablespoons
Grated American cheese	1 cup
Canned red pimentos	3
Hard-boiled eggs	4
Salt and pepper	To taste
Water	3 tablespoons

Chop onions and boil until transparent. Drain and cook in the oil and lard, being careful not to let it brown. Remove from fire and add grated cheese, chopped pimentos, chopped eggs, water, salt and pepper. Should the mixture be too dry you can add a little more oil.

CORPUS CHRISTI

AROUND the middle of May, we have the Corpus Christi Fiesta. It is frankly religious; but there are some typical customs attached to it.

Little boys and girls are dressed as Indian vendors and carry flowers, fruits, and even chickens and pigeons as offerings to church.

Natives sell little burros in the street with small crates filled with fruits and candy, decorated with flowers.

The origin of this brings us back to the early colonial days when railroads and paved highways did not exist. Natives from tropical towns in the southwest of the Republic came about this time of the year to sell their merchandise.

Around Corpus Christi Day, they could be seen entering Mexico City with their mules loaded with tropical fruits, cheese, molasses and confections of other kinds. They made their headquarters around the Cathedral, where they could sell their goods and, at the same time, enjoy the processions and other religious ceremonies.

A very special delicacy eaten that day is called:

GAZNATES (*Sweet Fritters*)

Pastry flour	2 cups (sifted)
Egg yolks	9
Shortening	1 teaspoon
Anise brandy	1 small glass

Mix the flour with the egg yolks and the shortening, then add the liqueur and knead thoroughly until very soft and smooth. Beat well against the table. Roll very thin on floured board and cut squares of about 3 inches. Take two opposite corners of each and seal, moistening ends. They should form small baskets.

Place some fat in the frying pan and heat very well. Hold the basket, or pastry tube, with two sticks and dip in the fat, turning the sticks quickly so as to keep the shape until light brown. Place on paper. The first one may seem a little hard to make but afterwards it is quite simple.

When cool, these Gaznates are filled with seven-minute frosting flavored with lemon or vanilla, or with Sweet Potato and Pineapple Dessert (page 165).

ST. JOHN'S DAY

(*Día de San Juan*)

ST. JOHN'S DAY is celebrated with festivities at the swimming pools and public baths. There is an old superstition that if a bath is taken on this day, your personal appearance improves, and your hair grows beautiful.

There is also the old tradition of dressing boys as soldiers, or at least buying them a casque or a soldier's cap and a stick with a horse head attached, which they can ride. This tradition is disappearing as many others are. When the army was not a permanent institution, especially during the years following the Conquest, each neighbor was given a piece of ground on which to build or plant — with the condition of keeping a horse and a gun ready to defend the government if necessary. On St. John's Day there was a parade or review, where all the men available went dressed as soldiers. Therefore the habit of calling "Juanes" (Johnnies) to the soldiers, and of dressing the boys as soldiers on St. John's Day.

Pears are very abundant at this time of the year. They sell them in bunches adorned with flowers, at the entrance of the public baths and swimming pools.

THE DAY OF ALL SOULS
(*Fiesta de Muertos*)

INSTEAD of Halloween we have the day of All Souls. At this time, toys and even candy are macabre, representing skeletons, tombs, etc. Hundreds of people go to the cemetery to take flowers to their dead ones.

This festival takes place on the 2nd of November, and although it should be a day of mourning, it is mixed with profane celebration.

In the big cities, people go to the cemeteries to take flowers to their departed relatives; but it is almost like a picnic, as they take food and even drinks.

In the bakeries they sell a special kind of coffee cake, that is eaten by everybody, even by the well-to-do people. They also sell skulls made of sugar and trimmed with small colored tinsel-paper figures and at times with names written on their foreheads. There is nothing morbid about this, as they just take the whole thing lightly.

In the Indian villages, the celebrations have much of the old superstitious idolatry. The tables are set with flowers (mostly marigolds) and food. The next morning the food is eaten by the family and neighbors; but they claim that it has no substance, because the dead ones came during the night and took it away.

But it is in Janitzio, the small island in the lake of Pátzcuaro, where this festival is best known, attracting every year visitors from the big cities, and many foreign tourists.

Two days before, all the men of the island go duck hunting in their canoes. These canoes are very picturesque, with their nets in the shape of butterfly wings. They hunt the ducks in the traditional form, with harpoons instead of guns.

The wives make tamales filled with duck meat cooked with chili sauce and in the evening they take a basket of them to the cemetery, together with big bouquets of marigolds, a frame in the shape of an arch to trim the tomb, and as many big candles as there are members of the family that have died. Only the women and the older children go to the cemetery. The men stay home to keep vigil, with the aid of black coffee and, of course, with liquor.

When the sun sets and darkness falls over the island, the sight is impressive, because the island itself is a small hill, and thus the cemetery on one of the sides, in a terrace-like arrangement, can be fully seen from the opposite shore. A sea of candles covers the cemetery.

In Pátzcuaro all the tourists stay up until late at night, or get up before dawn to watch the celebration.

In the morning the women and the children return to their homes and the whole family has a big meal of tamales and coffee or atole (a beverage made from cornmeal and flavored with chocolate or fruit juice).

There is a very special cake eaten that day:

ALL SOULS' DAY CAKE

Flour	3 cups
Yeast	1 cake
Butter	½ cup
Eggs	6
Orange blossom water	1 tablespoon
Anise extract	2 tablespoons
Salt	¼ teaspoon
Sugar	½ cup

Take ½ cup of the flour and mix it with the yeast dissolved in 3 tablespoons of lukewarm water. Make a dough and let it stand in warm place until double in bulk (10 to 15 minutes).

Sift the remaining flour three times. Make a hole in the flour. Place in the center the butter, the yeast dough, the egg yolks, the orange blossom water and the anise extract. Mix well with hands and add the egg whites little by little and only as necessary to make a soft dough. Beat it against the board until it forms bubbles and does not stick. Place the dough in a slightly greased pan covered with a napkin. Let stand in a warm place until double in bulk. Beat again and divide the dough in two parts. From each part take a piece of dough to form the "tears" (the shape of a long drop) to trim the cakes with. Place the cakes on baking sheets and let stand in warm place until double in bulk. Brush with egg, sprinkle with sugar and bake in hot oven 10 minutes. Reduce to medium and bake for about 20 minutes more or until perfectly baked.

BESIDES the festivals that are more or less general all over Mexico, each city has its own festival for its patron saint, with special customs, dances and food. In Puebla, for instance, there are several; but the principal one is that of San Sebastián.

In the suburb of that name, all around the church there are stands and even small provisional restaurants where they sell:

CHILES EN NOGADA
(Stuffed Peppers with Walnut Sauce)

The nuts are fresh at this time of the year (midwinter) and can be easily peeled; but the dish can be made by soaking the walnuts in hot water and peeling them. Or use blanched almonds and it is just as good.

Walnuts	50
Cream cheese	1 3-ounce package
Bread soaked in milk	1 slice
Salt, sugar and cinnamon	To taste
Green peppers	6
Eggs	3

STUFFING

Shortening	3 tablespoons
Ground veal	½ pound
Ground pork	½ pound
Tomatoes	3
Minced onion	1 tablespoon
Minced garlic	1 clove (optional)
Almonds	18
Raisins	18
Saffron	1 pinch
Banana	1 (optional)
Apple	1 (optional)
Peach	1 (optional)
Boiled minced ham	4 tablespoons
Sugar, cinnamon and ground clove	To taste
Salt	To taste

On the eve of making this dish soak the walnuts in hot water, take off the thin peeling, and place in cold water overnight.

Next day, one hour before serving, pass the nuts through fine food chopper (or pound in mortar). Mix well with the cheese and the soaked bread. If too thick, add a little milk until creamy. Season well with salt, sugar and cinnamon.

Boil the green peppers for 10 minutes. Discard the seeds and fill peppers with stuffing made as follows: Heat the shortening, add the veal and pork and when brown add the chopped tomatoes, onion and minced garlic. Cook for a few minutes, then add the blanched and chopped almonds, soaked raisins, saffron, peeled and chopped fruits, and ham. Season to taste and let dry.

Roll the stuffed peppers in flour. Beat the egg whites until stiff; add the yolks one by one and continue beating. Dip the peppers in this egg mixture and fry in hot fat.

Place on hot platter and serve with the cold sauce. In Mexico, they are served with pomegranate grains sprinkled on top.

Typically Texan Mexican Recipes

BY HELEN CORBITT

Texans have always enjoyed a South of the Border flavor in their food. There are no signs of weakening! They do, however, as in other things, have their own way of interpreting Mexican dishes. I would call these Typically Texan Mexican Recipes.

CHILI

Coarsely ground lean meat	3 pounds
Coarsely ground suet (optional)	½ cup
or salad oil	¼ cup
Chopped onion	1 cup
Garlic (chopped)	1 clove
or garlic powder	1 teaspoon

Chili powder	4 tablespoons
Ground cumin seed	1 tablespoon
Salt	1 tablespoon
Water	2 quarts
Chopped canned or fresh tomatoes	3 cups
Flour	2 tablespoons
Cornmeal	2 tablespoons

Brown beef in suet with onion and garlic. Add the chili powder, cumin, salt and water. Cook covered at low heat for 45 minutes. Add tomatoes and cook 30 minutes more. Add flour and cornmeal and cook until thickened. Serve with pinto beans, or with rice, or over broken soft tortillas with grated cheese and onion and baked at 350° until cheese is melted. For 12.

I have my own interpretation of Enchiladas, and have always found them highly acceptable.

MY ENCHILADAS

Tortillas	24
Chili	1 recipe
Grated Provolone cheese	2 cups
Chopped onion	1 cup
Cheddar-type cheese	2 cups

Keep tortillas warm in a damp towel or napkin. Skim off the fat from the chili and dip the tortillas in it. Mix half the cheese with the onion, and place about 2 tablespoons of the mixture in the center and roll up well (like an Enchilada, of course). Lay side by side in a shallow buttered casserole.

Bake in a 350° oven for 10 minutes. Cover with some of the chili and rest of the cheese. Run under broiler until cheese is melted.

There are few cocktail parties in Texas without:

CHILI CON QUESO

Chopped onion	1 cup
Chopped green pepper	¾ cup
Tomatoes (peeled and chopped)	2 cups
Butter	2 tablespoons
Salt	1 teaspoon
Pepper	1 teaspoon
Paprika	1 tablespoon
Flour	1 tablespoon
Processed cheese (grated)	2 pounds
Hot water	1 cup

Sauté onion, pepper and tomatoes in butter over a low flame until tender. Add seasoning, flour and cheese. Add hot water and cook slowly for 10 minutes. Serve over hot toasted tortillas, or use as a dip with potato chips or Fritos. Chopped Jalapeño peppers added to it give the "twang" that Texans like. Also some kind of Guacamole dip — and this variation is mild but good, and keeps its color — which I like (avocados turn dark when they are peeled).

GUACAMOLE

Cream cheese	1 3-ounce package
Sauterne	1 tablespoon
Avocados (mashed)	2
Garlic salt	¼ teaspoon
Curry powder	1 teaspoon
Salt and paprika	To taste
Tabasco	To taste

Mix the cream cheese with the sauterne and whip until light. Add rest of ingredients. Season with salt, paprika and a dash of Tabasco. Makes about 2 cups.

There are as many Tamale Pie recipes as there are Texans. Here are two.

CHICKEN TAMALE PIE

Sliced onion	1 cup
Olive oil	1 tablespoon
Kernel corn or freshly grated green corn	1½ cups
Pimento-stuffed olives	½ cup (sliced)
Browned almonds	½ cup
Garlic (chopped)	1 clove
Jalapeño chili	1 small can
Sugar	1 tablespoon
Chopped fresh or canned tomatoes	1½ cups
Grated processed cheese	2 cups
Diced chicken or turkey	2 cups
Tamales (canned, frozen or fresh from a Mexican factory)	24

Sauté the onions in the olive oil. Add rest of ingredients

One of my favorite dishes is called Chalupas. It is inexpensive, goes a long way, and is good for informal entertaining and picnics.

CHALUPAS

Chopped onion	1 cup
Butter or salad oil	2 tablespoons
Hamburger meat	1 pound
Flour	2 tablespoons
Chili powder	3 tablespoons
Water	1 cup
Tomato soup	1½ cups
Light cream	1½ cups
Salt	To taste
Tortillas	12
Grated American cheese	1½ cups

Sauté half the onions in butter until soft. Add hamburger meat and cook until brown. Add the flour and chili powder and cook five minutes more. Add water. Cover and simmer until thick. Mix soup, cream and rest of raw onion, and salt. Cut tortillas in strips and place in a buttered shallow casserole. Alternate with the meat and cheese mixtures until the casserole is filled, with cheese mixture on top. Bake at 325° until hot and browned. For 6 or 8.

Another good ole Texas recipe is:

CHILI AND HOMINY

Chopped onion	2 tablespoons
Garlic	1 clove
Butter	2 tablespoons
Ground beef	4 pounds
Chili powder	1 tablespoon
Bouillon	2 cups
Hominy (canned)	2 cups
Grated cheese	2 cups

Simmer the onion and garlic in the butter until soft. Add the beef, chili powder and bouillon and simmer. Mix with hominy. Place in a buttered casserole in layers alternating with the grated cheese. Bake at 350° for 45 minutes. For 8 or 10.

And:

HOMINY WITH RIPE OLIVES

Chopped onion	2 tablespoons
Butter	2 tablespoons
Flour	2 tablespoons
Milk	1 cup
Hominy (canned)	2 cups
Grated cheddar cheese	½ cup
Ripe olives (sliced)	½ cup
Paprika	

Sauté onion in the butter, add the flour. Cook until bubbly. Add the milk and cook until thick. Mix with the hominy, cheese and olives. Pour into buttered casserole. Sprinkle with paprika and bake at 350° for 35 minutes. For 4 or 6. And nice for brunch with ham and such.

Since chili is popular, the flavor of Texas Barbecue goes well with the young (both in age and in heart). I like to serve this for a cocktail party, when I feel poor, but my guests would never guess. I buy some half-dollar-size hamburger buns on special order, and let them all make their own. Also serve it on large toasted buns for a "fill them up" lunch or supper.

BARBECUED HAMBURGERS

Hamburger	5 pounds
Salad oil	⅓ cup
Chopped onion	2 cups
Sugar	2 tablespoons
Vinegar	1 cup
Catsup	3 cups
Chopped green peppers	2 cups
Salt	1 tablespoon
Dry mustard	½ cup

Brown meat in the oil until crumbly. Add rest of ingredients and cover. Simmer slowly for 1 hour. Watch it — it burns easily. For 20.

Of all Mexican food in Texas, the dish everyone tries to serve is a good Chili Rellenos (Stuffed Peppers). This is a tested restaurant recipe.

CHILI RELLENOS

Green peppers (large)	8
Chopped onion	½ cup
Tomato (peeled, chopped)	1
Ground beef	1 pound
Raisins	½ cup
Chopped pecans	½ cup
Salt and pepper	To taste
Eggs (separated)	2

Place peppers in a 400° oven until skins blister. Peel these skins off. Slit and remove seeds. Sauté the onion, tomatoes and beef until done. This mixture should be moist. Add the raisins and nuts. Season to your taste. Stuff the peppers with this mixture. Beat egg whites until stiff, add the egg yolks and mix. Dip stuffed peppers in milk, flour, then egg mixture. Fry in deep fat until golden brown. For 8. Serve hot with:

SPANISH SAUCE (3 cups)

Chopped onion	½ cup
Garlic	1 clove (crushed)
Diced celery (may be omitted)	½ cup
Diced green pepper	¼ cup
Olive oil	2 tablespoons
Canned tomatoes	2½ cups
Bay leaf	1
Salt	2 teaspoons
Sugar	2 teaspoons
Chopped parsley	2 teaspoons
Cloves	4
Flour	1 teaspoon

Sauté the onion, garlic, celery and green pepper in olive oil until soft, but not brown. Add remaining ingredients, except flour, and cook over low heat until thick. Remove garlic and cloves and add flour, dissolved in a little water. Use over meat loaf, cutlets, and with cooked shrimp over rice. Leftover sauce may be poured over canned green beans, okra, eggplant and like vegetables.

A really interesting salad to serve with a Mexican luncheon is this:

GUACAMOLE ASPIC

Large ripe avocados	2
Lemon juice	4 teaspoons
Minced onion	1 tablespoon
Salt	½ teaspoon
Chili sauce	1 tablespoon
Chopped green chiles	2 tablespoons
Gelatin, for each	1 tablespoon
Water	1 cup
Guacamole (p. 208)	2 cups

Mash the avocados, mix with the lemon juice, onion, salt, chili sauce and chilies. Dissolve the gelatin in the cold water and melt over hot water. When cold fold into the Guacamole. Pour into a ring mold and set aside to congeal. Turn out on a large tray and surround with salad greens and cherry tomatoes. For 6 to 8.

For the conservative side of Mexican cooking, Texans like:

RICE SPOON BREAD

Cooked rice	1 cup
Yellow cornmeal	¼ cup
Sour milk or buttermilk	2 cups
Baking soda	½ teaspoon
Salt	1 teaspoon
Eggs (beaten)	2
Melted bacon grease or butter	2 tablespoons

Mix above ingredients and place in greased baking dish. Bake 1 hour in 325° oven. 6 servings.

And:

SPANISH GRITS SOUFFLE

White hominy grits (uncooked)	1 cup
Milk	2½ cups
Butter	2 tablespoons
Chopped green pepper	2 tablespoons
Chopped pimento	2 tablespoons
Egg yolks	4
Salt	1 tablespoon
Egg whites	4

Cook grits and milk together until thick. Remove, add butter, green pepper and pimento. Cool. Add egg yolks and salt. Fold in well-beaten egg whites. Bake in a buttered 3-quart casserole at 350° for 30 minutes. For 6 or 8.

This grits dish is nice with scrambled eggs for a breakfast or supper dish, and wonderful with chicken hash.

A Mexican Dinner party can bring high praise to any hostess. When I was manager of the Houston Country Club "Mexican Buffet Night" was by far the most fun, and drew the most people. I always used a mixture of gay colored tablecloths. For candle holders, old bottles dripped with colored candle wax, with pennies inserted in them to make the drips more irregular and fantastic in shape. I decorated the Club with great bunches of green leaves that I daubed (or literally threw the paint on) with bright-hued water paints. So effective were they, when in all innocence I said I picked them from the shrubbery around the golf course, that some of the guests went hunting for them. Everything low in cost, but long in time of preparation — and always gay, *muy alegre,* with music and noise of all kinds — mostly happy relaxed conversation.

The menu could have been this:

Guacamole Dip with Fried Tortilla Strips

Enchiladas with Chili

Chili Rellenos with Spanish Sauce

Mexican Rice

Chili con Queso (to dribble over all!)

Hot Tortillas with Sweet Butter

Salad of Greens, Chunks of peeled ripe Tomatoes, Thin slices of Onion and raw Carrots with a clear French Dressing

A Tray of canned Pineapple Slices

Assorted Cheeses and Pralines, or any other sweet cooky — Maria de Carbia's Orange Sand Tart is great!

INDEX OF
ILLUSTRATIONS

INDEX

Index of Illustrations